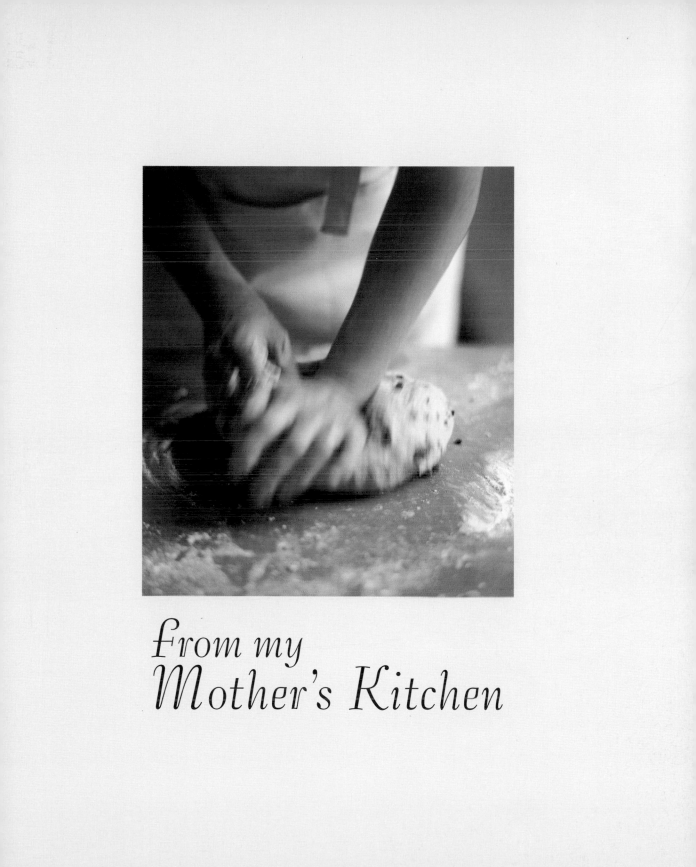

from my
Mother's Kitchen

From my Mother's Kitchen

simple recipes for classic comfort food

contributing editor
Jenny Linford

RYLAND
PETERS
& SMALL

LONDON NEW YORK

First published in the UK in 2009
by Ryland Peters & Small
20–21 Jockey's Fields
London WC1R 4BW
www.rylandpeters.com

10 9 8 7 6 5 4 3 2 1

Text © Fiona Beckett, Susannah Blake, Maxine
Clark, Linda Collister, Ross Dobson, Clare Ferguson,
Tonia George, Kate Habershon, Jennifer Joyce,
Jane Noraika, Louise Pickford, Sonia Stevenson,
Fran Warde, Laura Washburn, Lindy Wildsmith, and
Ryland Peters & Small 2009

Design and commissioned photographs
© Ryland Peters & Small 2009

Image taken from Weaving Patterns, published by
The Pepin Press, www.pepinpress.com: endpapers and
pages 3, 5 background, 15, 39, 59, 85, 111, 151

ISBN: 978 1 84597 817 4

A catalogue record for this book
is available from the British Library.

Printed and bound in China.

Designers Carl Hodson and Iona Hoyle
Editor Ann Baggaley
Production Manager Patricia Harrington
Art Director Leslie Harrington
Publishing Director Alison Starling

Indexer Hilary Bird

Notes

• All spoon measurements are level, unless otherwise
stated.

• Eggs are medium unless otherwise specified. Uncooked
or partially cooked eggs should not be served to the very
old, frail, young children, pregnant women or those with
compromised immune systems.

• Ovens should be preheated to the specified
temperature. Recipes in this book were tested using a
regular oven. If using a fan-assisted oven, follow the
manufacturer's instructions for adjusting temperatures.

Contents

introduction

The foods we eat as children often become 'comfort foods' later in life because they bring back happy memories of childhood and family or are associated with a particular place or time. Food is, of course, noted for its powers to evoke the past; the sensory act of tasting a dish or ingredient has the amazing ability to reconnect you very powerfully to times gone by. You might remember the favourite cake that your mother always made for your birthday or a real treat that was cooked only on special occasions for family celebrations. Often, the most vivid food memories are of simple things — the savoury taste of the gravy served with a Sunday roast, the satisfying sweetness of maple syrup soaking into pancakes warm from the frying pan, or the pleasurable, cool, slippery texture of a jelly eaten on a summer's day.

All around the world, the sharing of food is used to cement relationships, within both families and communities. The offering of food has been a fundamental element of human hospitality for centuries. Sitting down and eating a meal together is an important aspect of social life. Mealtimes are a simple but effective way to strengthen bonds within the family, bringing the people within a household together in a hospitable way to share food. Mealtimes offer the time and opportunity for people to talk to one another without distractions, to make those connections so important for a strong family. Sharing the table with their family offers children not simply the chance to learn polite table manners but also, at a more profound level, to learn about good social behaviour and how to respect others.

We still instinctively recognize the value of food cooked in the family home. It is no coincidence that in many cultures the phrase 'just like mother makes it' is the highest praise that can be bestowed upon a dish. 'Home-cooking' is a phrase that carries with it connotations of simplicity, but also of comfort and a sense of belonging. Homely food — the sort of food that simply isn't offered by either fast-food joints or smart restaurants — continues to retain an enormous appeal. Today, ready meals offer a quick-fix solution to the question 'What shall we eat tonight?' Many people, however, simply prefer to do their own cooking, taking pleasure from putting together a meal for their loved ones. This type of domestic cooking does not have to be sophisticated or complex to be enjoyed; in fact, simple, home-cooked dishes have their own, very special appeal.

In today's busy, pressurized world, where many parents juggle bringing up a family with the demands of a job, cooking can all too easily become a humdrum chore, yet another task that has to be fitted into a busy day. On the other hand, there is a great satisfaction to be had in feeding your family, cooking good, simple, tasty food and watching it being eaten with appetite and enjoyment. Eating is, of course, essential for existence. As a parent, there is a profound satisfaction in knowing that your family are eating a healthy, balanced diet and that you are contributing to their wellbeing in the most fundamental of ways.

For hundreds of years, cookery skills were passed on from one generation to another within families, with grandmothers or mothers teaching their granddaughters or daughters how to cook. Culinary skills, such as making bread, pastry or fresh pasta, are enjoyably learned by watching someone who knows what they're doing. Recipes, too, were traditionally often passed down. Most families have at least one inherited recipe, whether it is for something as simple as making successful, crunchy, roast potatoes for Sunday lunch or a favourite, indulgent trifle.

Cookbooks, of course, are often the starting point for many family favourites. You might be lucky enough to have a battered copy of your mother's favourite cookbook, complete with pencilled notes in the margin on how the recipes worked; if so, treasure it as an heirloom, as by cooking from it you will have a wonderful window into the past. The recipes gathered together for this cookbook are all classics, chosen for their simplicity and accessibility. These recipes are not designed to 'show off' your expertise, but they are all about producing delicious food simply. This collection of traditional recipes offers a chance to cook dishes that will appeal to your family and friends and form a great foundation for your own home-cooking.

Looking back to how our mothers and our mothers' mothers shopped for food and cooked, there are some simple but valuable ideas that we can benefit from following.

*top ten tips from
mother's kitchen*

1 *Eat together.* Eating together is a great way to cement relationships, providing an opportunity for the family to share time and conversation and laughter. This is particularly important in today's increasingly fragmented world, where things such as personal computers and electronic media offer the chance to beguile away the time on one's own. Sitting down and sharing a meal with your loved ones is a simple and pleasurable way to connect with them.

2 *Cook with children.* In the age of microwaves and ready meals, cookery skills that were once taken for granted are being lost alarmingly quickly. Cooking with children is a great, effective way to pass on food knowledge and basic cookery skills. Of course, you don't want to make the cooking a chore. Give the child or children helping you straightforward, do-able tasks like sifting flour into a mixing bowl, weighing out the butter for a cake or whisking egg whites until stiff, the latter task a lovely glimpse into the alchemy of cooking. Engage their senses by asking your children to sniff at the spices you need for a dish or to pick fresh herbs from the garden, so that they learn to identify herbs and spices through what they look like and by their distinctive smells.

3 *Celebrate seasonality.* Return to seasonal food shopping. Today, we live in a world where most ingredients are available all the time, albeit at a price. Fruits, such as strawberries and raspberries, that were once an annual summer treat, can now be found during the winter months, flown in from the other side of the world. Eating fresh fruits and vegetables when they are in season locally makes a lot of sense, as they are at their best and cheapest. A recently harvested apple, for

example, is a world away in terms of texture and flavour from an apple that's been stored for many months. By shopping seasonally you learn to appreciate the natural rhythms of the seasons and to enjoy the contrast between these different times of the year in terms of what is available. Treats such as the first asparagus or cherries of the season take on a new and special significance.

4 *Stock up the freezer*. With a little forethought and planning, it's a simple matter to cook double quantities of dishes such as stews or pasta sauces, then batch them up and freeze them for future use. These frozen dishes make a great fallback on busy days when you don't have time to cook from scratch but still want to eat homemade food. It's also very useful to have a few handy ingredients, such as minced meat or chicken breast fillets, in the freezer, in case you need to cook an extra meal and don't have time for a trip to the shops.

5 *Embrace good housekeeping!* For centuries housekeeping skills, the ability to make the most of what one had, were highly valued. Today, at least in the more affluent parts of the world, we live in wasteful times. It is well worth taking note of the more careful approach to cooking that earlier generations took. Once you've enjoyed a meal of roast chicken, for example, use the carcass of the chicken to make a flavoursome stock by simmering it in water with an onion, carrot and a few herbs. It's incredibly simple and so much tastier than stock cube stock, and the homemade stock can then be used as the base for risottos, soups and numerous other dishes. Bear in mind that a little forward planning makes cooking much less stressful. Work out what you are going to cook for the next few meals and shop accordingly. One simple way

to get ahead is to make a stew or pasta sauce a day or so in advance, then chill it until required. An advantage to this is that many dishes actually improve in flavour if they are left for a while before eating.

6 *Support local food shops*. Shopping locally for your food at independent food shops is a great way of connecting to your community. If you are lucky enough to have a good butcher, fishmonger or a greengrocer near where you live or work, then it is well worth cultivating a relationship with them. A good butcher, for example, will have a range of items that supermarkets simply do not carry, such as bones for stock or cheaper cuts of meat. He will also be able to prepare meat for you, such as boning out a shoulder of lamb. You might have a favourite bakery, cheesemonger or delicatessen; if so, make sure to support them by shopping at them rather than automatically doing your entire food shop in a supermarket. Buying good things to eat from these shops — a decent loaf of bread, a piece of artisan cheese or some quality sliced meat or olives — makes cooking and eating at home a pleasure.

7 *Discover markets*. Going to a market once a week was a traditional way of food shopping. Hunt out your nearest traditional street market or a farmers' market, which showcases seasonal produce from local farms. The benefits of shopping at a good market is that prices are competitive and the produce noticeably fresh. Shopping at markets is a sociable occupation, which brings with it not only the fun of finding bargains but also of chatting to stallholders who are likely to be food enthusiasts. Ask them, or the other customers, for advice on how to deal with such things as a type of fish you've never cooked or a vegetable you have never tried.

8 *Try baking at home.* There is no doubt that baked goods taste infinitely better when they are just cooked. And that wonderful flavour, of course, is the true reward of home baking. There is nothing really very difficult or complicated about baking. Once you have mastered a few basics, such as how to use yeast or judge when you have kneaded dough long enough, then there are so many delicious things to make, both sweet and savoury. It is hard to beat a crusty loaf of freshly baked bread, so good that you keep coming back for yet another slice, or scones served warm from the oven, or a crispy golden piecrust. An added extra is the wonderful smell of bread or a cake baking, a lovely, comforting aroma that entices everyone into the kitchen.

9 *Have a go at home preserving.* For centuries, people preserved food such as meat, fruit and vegetables in order to survive harsh, cold winters, when fresh food was scarce. Today, we don't need to preserve food in the way that we used to. There is a real satisfaction to be had, however, in making the most of nature's bounty when it's plentiful. Markets or pick-your-own farms, where you harvest fruit and vegetables, are a great way of getting seasonal produce in bulk. Try making a jar of sweet, red strawberry jam or tangy marmalade to serve at breakfast or transforming vegetables into tasty pickles, relishes and chutneys to go with cold meats. You are guaranteed a quiet glow of pride when you serve these to family or friends.

10 *Look after your larder.* Cooking is much simpler and more enjoyable if your larder is well stocked to start with. Make sure you have essential staples from which you can construct a meal. Rice, pasta, dried pulses and tinned tomatoes are all great standbys when you need to feed the family in a hurry and have only a few leftovers to work with. The same principle applies to condiments and other flavourings. Make sure you have good olive oil and vinegar, mustard, garlic, root ginger and an assortment of spices to hand as this enables you to cook a huge range of dishes without the bother of tracking down the ingredients specially. Once you have made the initial investment, many of these ingredients will last for months and prove invaluable.

wholesome salads
& tasty sides

Crisp lettuce, crumbly feta cheese, fragrant herbs, vinegary olives and salty anchovies thrown together in a bowl – Greek salad is not only healthy but also easy to make. Use unstoned Kalamata olives, if possible, as they have more flavour than other kinds.

greek salad

Put the lettuce in a large bowl. Add the cheese, olives, onions, cucumbers and tomatoes.

To make the dressing, put the olive oil, lemon juice, salt and pepper in a jug or bowl and beat with a fork, then pour over the salad. Alternatively, sprinkle the dressing ingredients onto the salad separately.

Top the salad with the anchovies, oregano and mint, and serve.

note: Look out for big cans of salted anchovies in Greek markets and delicatessens – wheels of whole fish arranged nose to tail, which need to be rinsed and filleted. If these are unavailable, use canned anchovy fillets.

1 iceberg lettuce, quartered and torn apart

about 250 g feta cheese, crumbled into big pieces or cut into cubes

about 200 g Kalamata olives

2 red onions, thinly sliced

2 mini cucumbers, halved lengthways, then thinly sliced diagonally

4 large tomatoes, cut into chunks

8 anchovy fillets, or to taste (see note)

a few sprigs of oregano, torn

a few sprigs of mint, torn

dressing

6 tablespoons extra virgin olive oil

2 tablespoons freshly squeezed lemon juice

sea salt and freshly ground black pepper

serves 4

This is one of the classic salads. There is much pontificating about the most authentic ingredients, but you can use whatever you like from the basic list. Arrange in circles on a large platter or offer single servings.

salade niçoise

Cook the baby potatoes in boiling salted water until tender, about 10 minutes. Drain and plunge them into a bowl of iced water. Let cool. Drain, then toss in a little olive oil and cut in half.

Put the eggs in a saucepan of cold water, bring to the boil, reduce the heat and simmer for 5 minutes. Drain, then cover with cold water and leave to cool. Peel and cut in half just before serving the salad.

Steam the broad beans and green beans separately until tender. Plunge into iced water, then pop each broad bean out of its grey skin. Alternatively, microwave the broad beans on HIGH for 3 minutes if fresh or 2 minutes if frozen, then refresh in iced water and peel as before. Microwave the green beans for 2 minutes, then plunge into iced water as before.

Blanch the spring onions for 30 seconds in boiling water. Drain and plunge into the iced water. Alternatively, leave uncooked, but trim and halve lengthways.

Thinly slice the red onions and cucumbers, Slice the cucumbers diagonally. If peeling the peppers, do so using a vegetable peeler, then cut off the top and bottom, open out, deseed and cut the flesh into thick strips.

Put the lettuce leaves on a platter. Add bundles of green beans and spring onions, then the potatoes, halved eggs, tomatoes, cucumber, onions and peppers. Top with anchovy fillets or tuna, black olives, caperberries or capers and basil leaves. Mix the vinaigrette ingredients in a small jug and serve separately.

10–12 small salad potatoes, such as Pink Fir Apples or Charlottes

extra virgin olive oil, for tossing the potatoes

4 small eggs

100 g shelled broad beans, fresh or frozen

100 g green beans, stalks trimmed

3 spring onions, halved lengthways

2 small red onions, halved lengthways

2 mini cucumbers, unwaxed

2 red or yellow peppers, peeled (see method)

4 Little Gem baby lettuces

1 punnet cherry tomatoes, about 20, halved

1 small can anchovy fillets, drained

1 large can of good-quality tuna, drained

about 20 Niçoise black olives

about 20 caperberries or 3 tablespoons salt-packed capers, rinsed and drained

a large handful of fresh basil leaves

vinaigrette

6 tablespoons extra virgin olive oil

1 tablespoon white wine vinegar, cider vinegar or sherry vinegar

1 teaspoon Dijon mustard (optional)

1 garlic clove, crushed

sea salt and freshly ground black pepper

serves 8 as a starter, 4 as a main course

This is probably the most famous salad in the world, with the perfect combination of salty, crispy crunch. Note that this recipe serves one person – to serve more, just multiply the ingredients according to the number of people you have at the table.

caesar salad

To cook the egg, put it in a small saucepan, cover with water and bring to the boil. Reduce the heat and simmer for 4–5 minutes. Remove from the heat and cover with cold water to stop it cooking further. Let cool a little, then peel. Cut into quarters just before serving.

To make the croutons, tear the bread into bite-sized chunks, brush with oil or butter and rub with the garlic. Cook on a preheated stove-top grill pan until the croutons are crisply golden and barred with brown.

Put the lettuce in a large bowl and sprinkle with salt and pepper, add the lemon juice and toss with your hands. Sprinkle with olive oil and toss again to coat the leaves.

Put the croutons in a bowl and put the dressed leaves on top. Add the anchovies, egg and Parmesan, sprinkle with pepper and serve with lemon wedges, if using.

note: Traditionally, the dressing for caesar salad uses a raw egg yolk (see the alternative method on page 165). However, as some people are advised not to eat uncooked eggs, the recipe above has been adapted.

1 egg

6 smallest leaves of cos lettuce (a young cos, not Little Gem)

½ tablespoon freshly squeezed lemon juice, plus 1 lemon cut into wedges, to serve (optional)

2 tablespoons extra virgin olive oil

3–4 canned anchovy fillets, rinsed and drained

Parmesan cheese, at room temperature, shaved into curls with a vegetable peeler

sea salt and freshly ground black pepper

croutons

1 thick slice crusty white bread or challah bread

2 tablespoons oil and/or butter, for cooking

1 garlic clove, crushed

serves 1

In America, this salad is known as 'mesclun' (from the same origin as the word 'miscellaneous'). In Italian, it's *insalata di campo* – 'little salad of the fields'. Choose a combination of leaves – some crisp, some bitter, some peppery, some soft – and sprigs of scented herbs. The perfection of the dressing is what's important.

mixed green salad

Wash the leaves as necessary and dry in a salad spinner. Put into plastic bags or wrap in dry tea towels and chill for at least 30 minutes to crisp the leaves. (If washing soft leaves like rocket, do it at the last minute, otherwise they will go mushy. Most supermarkets sell them in bags, already washed and dried.)

If using garlic, put it on a board with a pinch of sea salt and crush thoroughly with the back of a heavy knife (this gives a better texture than using a garlic crusher). Transfer to a salad bowl, add the olive oil, vinegar, mustard, if using, and pepper, then beat with a fork or small whisk. Add extra salt and pepper, to taste.

When ready to serve, add the leaves and turn them gently in the dressing until lightly coated. (Use your hands, so as not to bruise the leaves and to make sure every one is well coated.) Alternatively, if you have used a large proportion of soft leaves, serve the salad undressed, with the dressing in a small jug. The salad can then be dressed just before eating.

note: A few tablespoons of dressing is plenty for a salad of this size – too much will spoil it. A gentle vinegar works best (especially white rice vinegar or sherry vinegar).

your choice of:

crisp leaves, such as Little Gem

soft leaves, such as oak leaf lettuce

peppery leaves, such as watercress or nasturtium leaves or flowers

bitter leaves, such as dandelion or chicory

rocket and wild rocket

soft herb sprigs, such as fennel, parsley or basil

dressing

½ garlic clove (optional)

a pinch of sea salt flakes

6 parts extra virgin olive oil

1 part vinegar, such as cider, white rice, sherry, white wine or red wine

1 teaspoon Dijon mustard (optional)

freshly ground black pepper

serves 4–6

An ideal – and healthy – accompaniment to most main meals, especially roast meats, this dish is especially versatile because it can be made with a variety of greens, including baby chard, spinach, mustard greens or rocket. Simply use whatever happens to be in season. Use one of the suggested methods below, whichever suits you best.

wilted greens

method one (best for larger, robust greens, such as baby chard):

Bring a large saucepan of water to the boil. Salt well, add the greens and blanch for 2–3 minutes. Drain and refresh under cold running water. Leave to dry in a colander, tossing occasionally to let all the water escape (squeeze excess with your hands if necessary). To serve, sprinkle with 2–3 tablespoons olive oil, the juice of ½ lemon and a good sprinkling of salt and pepper.

method two (best for smaller leaves, such as baby spinach, rocket and mixed baby greens):

Crush the garlic clove, but leave whole and spear on the end of a fork. Heat about 2 tablespoons olive oil in a large pan. Add a very large handful of leaves and cook, stirring with the garlic fork, until wilted. Using tongs, transfer the leaves to a large plate and continue adding handfuls until all the greens are wilted. Season with a trickle of extra oil, a squeeze of lemon juice and a good sprinkling of salt and pepper.

750 g greens, mixed or single, such as baby chard, spinach, mustard greens or rocket

extra virgin olive oil

1 lemon

1 garlic clove, peeled (see method two)

fine sea salt and freshly ground black pepper

serves 2–4

One of the delights of cooking with mushrooms, especially the chestnut variety, is that their flavour is so good you need add very few other ingredients. That said, the perfect partners for mushrooms are garlic and cream, a truly sublime combination.

garlic mushrooms in white wine and cream

Put the oil, butter and garlic in a large saucepan and heat until the butter melts. Stir in the mushrooms and cook for 5–10 minutes until they have softened.

Add the wine and cream and bring to the boil. Reduce the heat slightly and continue cooking until the liquid has reduced by half. Season to taste, stir in the parsley and serve.

note: The best way to crush garlic is to add a pinch of salt then crush it with the back of a heavy knife or a mortar and pestle. The salt draws out the juices to make a pulp.

1 tablespoon extra virgin olive oil

50 g unsalted butter

3 garlic cloves, crushed

500 g chestnut mushrooms, thickly sliced

100 ml white wine

4 tablespoons double cream

sea salt and freshly ground black pepper

a bunch of flat leaf parsley, finely chopped

serves 4

These firm but juicy tomatoes burst with the flavour of the sun. They take no time to prepare, but need a long time in the oven and smell fantastic while cooking. Plum tomatoes have less moisture and work well, but you can use any vine-ripened variety, just as long as they have some taste!

slow-roasted tomatoes with garlic and oregano

Preheat the oven to 160°C (325°F) Gas 3.

Cut the tomatoes in half lengthways (around the middle if using round tomatoes). Put them cut side up on the baking sheet.

Put the garlic, oregano, olive oil, salt and pepper in a bowl and mix well, then spoon or brush the mixture over the cut tomatoes.

Bake in the preheated oven for 1½–2 hours, checking every now and then. The tomatoes should be slightly shrunk but still brilliantly red after cooking (if they are too dark, they will have a bitter flavour).

Serve topped with fresh basil leaves as an accompaniment to grills and fish, or use as a topping on bruschetta.

6–10 ripe tomatoes

2 garlic cloves, finely chopped

1 tablespoon dried oregano

4 tablespoons extra virgin olive oil

sea salt and freshly ground black pepper

fresh basil leaves, to serve

a baking sheet covered with greaseproof paper

serves 4

Every good roast needs the traditional accompaniments to take it to the next level of deliciousness. Roast potatoes are always a favourite at the Sunday lunch table. This method ensures that the potatoes emerge from the oven crispy outside and light inside – just as they should be!

roast potatoes

12–16 potatoes, peeled

4 tablespoons duck or goose fat,
or extra virgin olive oil

serves 4

Preheat the oven to 180°C (350°F) Gas 4.

Parboil the potatoes in salted boiling water for 12 minutes, then drain and shake in the colander to roughen up the outsides.

Heat the fat or oil in a large roasting tin in the oven and, when very hot, carefully add the potatoes, turning to coat them thoroughly. Return to the oven and cook for 40 minutes. Do not disturb them before that or you will spoil their chances of crisping up. Turn them and cook for another 20 minutes.

The secret of perfect mash is using a floury variety of potato that fluffs up properly. Older potatoes work better than new. This dish can be kept warm in the oven – 120°C (250°F) Gas ½ – for up to 2 hours if covered with buttered foil. Otherwise, cool and reheat gently, beating in extra melted butter and hot milk. If adding herbs, beat in just before serving.

mashed potatoes

750 g floury potatoes, quartered

55 g unsalted butter

75–100 ml milk

sea salt and freshly ground black pepper

serves 4

Put the potatoes in a saucepan of salted cold water and bring to the boil. As soon as the water boils, reduce to a simmer (it's important not to cook the potatoes too quickly) and cook for about 20 minutes. When perfectly done, the point of a sharp knife should glide into the centre of the potatoes.

Drain in a colander, then set over the hot pan to steam and dry out. Tip the potatoes back into the hot pan and crush with a potato masher or pass them through a mouli or ricer into the pan. Melt the butter in the milk. Using a wooden spoon, beat the butter and milk into the mash – an electric hand-mixer sometimes helps here. Season, pile into a warm dish and serve.

variation: spring onion and horseradish mash

Beat into the mash 3 tablespoons chopped spring onions sautéed in butter and 2 tablespoons creamed horseradish.

Yorkshire pudding used to be served at the beginning of a main meal to fill people up and make meat 'go further'. These days, it acts as a mop for gravy and pan juices from a roast. If you have any leftovers, the pudding is delicious next day with bacon for breakfast. Once you've made fresh horseradish sauce, the bottled variety will never be good enough. Grating the horseradish will make your eyes water, but the result is worth it.

yorkshire puddings and horseradish sauce

Preheat the oven to 230°C (450°F) Gas 8.

Put the milk, eggs, flour and salt in a bowl and whisk well.

Heat the oil or fat on top of the stove in one large tin or divide between a 6-hole tin (1 tablespoon fat for each hole) or a 12-hole tin (½ teaspoon fat for each hole). Pour in the batter (take care because it will spatter). Cook in the oven until well risen (35 minutes for the large tin or 15 minutes for the individual tins). Serve as soon as possible.

To make the horseradish sauce, scrape the fresh horseradish root clean and grate it finely to give 2 tablespoons. Put in a bowl, add the vinegar and salt and stir well. Add the cream and whisk until it becomes thick and light. Rest the sauce at room temperature for at least 2 hours, but serve the same day.

275 ml milk

2 whole eggs

125 g plain flour

½ teaspoon sea salt

4–6 tablespoons cooking oil, or fat from the roasting tin

a roasting tin 45 x 30 cm, or a 6 hole Yorkshire pudding tin, or a 12-hole muffin tin

serves 6

horseradish sauce

1 large horseradish root

1 tablespoon white wine vinegar

250 ml double cream

sea salt

makes about 500–600 m

These roasted vegetables make a tasty and colourful side dish with all the warmth of the Mediterranean sun. They are particularly delicious served with fish, but you can serve them to accompany meat dishes as well. Preparation couldn't be simpler and the vegetables need only occasional attention while they are cooking.

roasted mediterranean vegetables

Preheat the oven to 200°C (400°F) Gas 6.

Put the courgettes, peppers, onions and aubergine in a large roasting tin. Pour the oil over the vegetables, add a few drops of balsamic vinegar and toss well. Roast in the preheated oven for about 35–40 minutes, carefully turning twice, adding the thyme 10 minutes before the vegetables are cooked.

The vegetables should begin to take on colour and be tender but not disintegrating. Season them well with salt and pepper and transfer to a serving dish. Add the torn basil and serve.

3 small courgettes, halved or quartered

1 medium red pepper, quartered and deseeded

1 medium yellow pepper, quartered and deseeded

2 medium red onions, cut into 8 wedges through the root (keep the roots intact)

1 small aubergine, cut into large cubes

150 ml extra virgin olive oil

a few drops balsamic vinegar

2 sprigs of thyme

fresh basil leaves, torn

sea salt and freshly ground black pepper

serves 4

Messy and delicious, grilled sweetcorn dripping with butter is a particular favourite with a crowd of hungry youngsters. The chilli and lime add unusual and lively flavours to this summer barbecue classic. Serve with lots of paper napkins – this is definitely a hands-on dish.

barbecued sweetcorn with chilli lime butter

Preheat a barbecue or grill.

To make the chilli lime butter, put the chilli sauce, lime zest and butter in a bowl and beat well. Season with salt and pepper, then roll into a cylinder between sheets of damp greaseproof paper. Twist the ends firmly and chill for at least 1 hour until hard.

To barbecue the corn, melt the butter in a small saucepan and whisk in the chilli powder and lime juice. This will be the basting sauce for the corn.

Cook the corn on the preheated barbecue or grill for at least 10 minutes, basting and turning until golden brown all over, soft and lightly charred. Slice the chilled butter into disks and serve with the hot grilled corn.

12 ears of corn-on-the-cob, husked

125 g unsalted butter, melted

a large pinch of chilli powder

juice of 2 unwaxed limes (use the zest for the butter, see below)

sea salt and freshly ground black pepper

chilli lime butter

1 teaspoon sweet chilli sauce

finely grated zest 2 unwaxed limes

125 g unsalted butter, softened

serves 6

homely soups
& basic broths

beef stock · chicken stock · fish stock · vegetable stock
· tomato soup · cream of mushroom soup · leek and
potato soup with watercress purée · chicken noodle
soup · minestrone · scotch broth · french onion soup

A deeply flavoured beef stock makes all the difference to a finished sauce. Beef blade is available on or off the bone, but for a particularly flavoursome stock, buy it on the bone.

beef stock

4 tablespoons extra virgin olive oil

2 kg beef blade, cut into chunks

3 large onions, chopped

4 carrots, chopped

4 celery sticks, chopped

1 bouquet garni (page 41)

2 teaspoons sea salt

makes approximately 2 litres

Heat the olive oil in a large stockpot and fry the beef blade in several batches until well browned.

Add the remaining ingredients and 4 litres cold water and bring slowly to the boil, skimming the surface to remove the scum. Partially cover the pot and simmer gently for 3–4 hours until the stock is reduced by half and full of flavour. Season to taste.

Strain the stock through a fine sieve and leave to cool, then refrigerate for up to 3 days.

When you are ready to use the stock, remove the thick layer of fat from the surface.

variation: **meat glaze**

Return the strained stock to a clean pan and simmer until reduced to approximately 300 ml. Leave to cool. Refrigerate for up to 1 month.

Delicate soups and savoury sauces benefit from a good, homemade chicken stock base. Refrigerating the cold stock overnight allows the fat to solidify on the surface, making it much easier to remove.

chicken stock

To make the bouquet garni, remove the outer layer of leek (reserving the rest for the stock) and open out flat. Put the celery, garlic, bay leaves, parsley, thyme and peppercorns on top of the leek skin, then roll up tightly. Tie up with kitchen string.

Put the chicken in a large stockpot with all the remaining ingredients and cover with cold water (about 2 litres).

Bring slowly to the boil, skimming the surface to remove the scum. Partially cover the pot and simmer gently for 3 hours.

Strain the stock through a fine sieve and leave to cool, then refrigerate overnight.

Remove the thick layer of fat from the surface. Refrigerate for up to 3 days.

note: If preferred, you can wrap the bouquet garni in muslin instead of leek skin.

2-kg chicken, washed

2 onions, chopped

2 carrots, chopped

2 celery sticks, chopped

2 leeks, chopped

2 garlic cloves, peeled

1 bouquet garni (see below)

2 teaspoons sea salt

makes approximately 2 litres

bouquet garni

7.5-cm length of leek (see note)

7.5-cm length of celery stick

1 garlic clove, peeled

2 fresh bay leaves (or 1 dried)

2 fresh flat leaf parsley sprigs

2 fresh thyme sprigs

6 black peppercorns

These two stocks will keep well in the fridge for a few days and are economical to make. Most fishmongers will happily give you their fish trimmings and you can use up the left-overs in your vegetable basket.

fish stock

Wash the fish trimmings and put in a large saucepan with all the remaining ingredients and 1.5 litres cold water. Bring to the boil, skimming the surface to remove the scum. Partially cover the pan and simmer gently for 30 minutes (no longer, or you will get a bitter flavour).

Strain the stock through a fine sieve into a clean pan and return to the boil. Simmer, uncovered, for 15 minutes, or until the liquid is reduced by half. You should be left with approximately 1.25 litres fish stock. Leave to cool and refrigerate for up to 3 days.

1 kg fish trimmings

750 ml dry white wine

1 tablespoon white wine vinegar

2 large carrots, chopped

1 onion, chopped

2 celery sticks, chopped

1 leek, chopped

2 garlic cloves, peeled

1 bouquet garni (page 41)

1 teaspoon sea salt

makes approximately 1.25 litres

vegetable stock

Heat the olive oil in a large saucepan and fry the garlic, onion and leek for 10 minutes. Add the carrots, potatoes and celery and fry for a further 10 minutes, or until softened but not coloured.

Add the wine and boil rapidly for 2–3 minutes, or until the liquid is almost completely reduced. Add the remaining ingredients and 1.75 litres cold water and bring to the boil. Cover and simmer for 1 hour.

Strain the stock through a fine sieve and leave to cool completely. Refrigerate for up to 3 days.

2 tablespoons extra virgin olive oil

2 garlic cloves, peeled

1 onion, roughly chopped

1 large leek, chopped

2 carrots, chopped

2 potatoes, diced

2 celery sticks, chopped

150 ml dry white wine

1 ripe tomato, chopped

125 g mushrooms, chopped

50 g red lentils

1 bouquet garni (page 41)

2 teaspoons sea salt

makes approximately 1.75 litres

The ultimate home comfort, tomato soup needs to be made with really ripe, flavourful tomatoes – the best you can find. The citrus tang of the lemon will cut through the smoothness of the soup. Add some pesto and extra basil leaves to serve, for an Italian twist.

tomato soup

To skin the tomatoes, cut a cross in the base of each and dunk into a saucepan of boiling water. Remove after 10 seconds and put in a strainer set over a large saucepan. Slip off and discard the skins and cut the tomatoes in half around their 'equators'. Using a teaspoon, scoop out the seeds into the strainer, then press the pulp and juice through the strainer and transfer to a blender. Discard the seeds. Chop the tomato halves and add to the blender.

Purée the tomatoes, adding a little of the stock to help the process – you may have to work in batches. Add the remaining stock, season to taste with salt and pepper and transfer to the saucepan. Heat well without boiling. Serve in heated soup plates and top each serving with 1 teaspoon lemon juice, 1 tablespoon pesto (if using), chives or basil, lemon zest and pepper.

1 kg very ripe red tomatoes

500 ml chicken stock (page 41), or to taste

sea salt and coarsely crushed black pepper

to serve

shredded zest and freshly squeezed juice of 1 unwaxed lemon

4 tablespoons pesto (optional) (page 164)

scissor-snipped chives or torn basil

serves 4

You could make this soup with any cultivated mushrooms, but the dried porcini and large portobello mushrooms used here give a wonderful flavour and particularly rich colour. Most supermarkets stock a variety of fresh and dried mushrooms, so you can choose what you like.

cream of mushroom soup

Put the dried porcini in a bowl, add 250 ml boiling water and leave to soak for at least 15 minutes. Heat the oil in a frying pan, add the fresh mushrooms and sauté until coloured but still firm. Reserve a few slices for serving.

Add the onion to the frying pan and sauté until softened, then add the garlic, nutmeg and parsley. Rinse any grit out of the porcini and strain their soaking liquid several times through muslin or a tea strainer. Add the liquid and the porcini to the pan. Bring to the boil, then transfer to a food processor. Add 2 ladles of the boiling stock, then pulse until the mixture is creamy but still chunky.

Heat the butter in a saucepan until melted, stir in the flour and cook gently, stirring constantly, until the mixture is very dark brown (take care or it will burn). Add the remaining stock, 1 ladle at a time, stirring well after each addition. Add the mushroom mixture, bring to the boil, then simmer for 20 minutes. Season with salt and pepper to taste. Serve in heated soup bowls topped with a few reserved mushrooms, parsley and crème fraîche.

note: If you use a blender to make soup, the purée will be very smooth. If you use a food processor, it will be less smooth, and if you use the pulse button, you can make the mixture quite chunky, which suits mushrooms.

25 g dried porcini mushrooms

4 tablespoons extra virgin olive oil

6 large portobello mushrooms, wiped, trimmed and sliced

1 onion, halved and thinly sliced

3 garlic cloves, crushed

pinch of freshly grated nutmeg

leaves from a large bunch of fresh parsley, finely chopped in a food processor

1.25 litres boiling chicken stock (page 41) or vegetable stock (page 43)

4 tablespoons butter

4 tablespoons plain flour

sea salt and freshly ground black pepper

to serve

4–6 tablespoons coarsely chopped fresh parsley

4–6 tablespoons crème fraîche

serves 4–6

This is a gorgeously smooth and velvety soup that will suit all tastes and any family occasion, from picnics to dinner parties. To ensure a really smooth texture, it is very important to blend, then sieve the soup before serving. It is equally delicious served either hot or chilled.

leek and potato soup with watercress purée

To make the watercress purée, put the watercress leaves in a blender with the olive oil. Blend until smooth. Pour into a screwtop jar and set aside until needed.

To make the soup, melt the butter in a large saucepan and add the onions and leeks. Stir well, add 3 tablespoons water, cover tightly and cook over gentle heat for 10 minutes, or until soft and golden, but not at all brown.

Stir in the potatoes and chicken stock. Bring to the boil, reduce the heat, cover and simmer for 20 minutes, or until the potatoes are tender. Stir in the milk, then purée in a blender or with a handheld blender. Press the purée through a sieve, then return it to the pan. Stir in the crème fraîche and season. Leave to cool and chill (if serving chilled, add extra seasoning) or serve hot in warm soup bowls with a swirl of watercress purée and dollop of chilled crème fraîche.

75 g unsalted butter

2 onions, finely chopped

500 g leeks (white part only), finely chopped

175 g floury potatoes, chopped

1.35 litres chicken stock (page 41)

300 ml milk

150 ml crème fraîche, plus extra to serve

sea salt and freshly ground white pepper

watercress purée

125 g watercress, stalks removed

5 tablespoons extra virgin olive oil

serves 6

The trick to producing an extra rich stock for this soup is to brown the chicken first and cover while simmering. The result is a deep, flavoursome base that suits any additions. Fine egg noodles are classic for this comforting soup, but you can try rice or matzo balls.

chicken noodle soup

Heat 1 tablespoon of the olive oil in a large, heavy stockpot. Season the chicken pieces and brown them in the stockpot in batches. Put all the chicken pieces back in the pot with the onion, carrot, garlic and celery, and cook over low heat for 15 minutes. Pour in 1.5 litres water, add the bouquet garni and simmer, covered, for 1 hour over medium/low heat. Remove any foamy scum from the surface during cooking.

Strain the finished stock through a fine sieve into a bowl and skim off any excess fat. Reserve the chicken and let cool before removing the meat from the bones and roughly chopping it.

To finish, heat the remaining olive oil in a saucepan. Add the onion, carrots and celery, and season. Sauté for 5 minutes, then pour in the stock. Bring to the boil and add the noodles. Cook until the noodles are al dente, then add the chopped chicken. Sprinkle in the chopped parsley, stir and serve.

2 tablespoons olive oil

1.5 kg chicken drumsticks and thighs

1 medium onion, chopped

1 carrot, peeled and chopped

1 garlic clove, sliced

2 celery sticks, chopped

1 bouquet garni (page 41)

to finish

1 medium onion, chopped

2 large carrots, peeled and sliced 1 cm thick

2 celery sticks, sliced 2 cm thick

90 g fine egg noodles, broken into pieces

20 g fresh flat leaf parsley, finely chopped

sea salt and freshly ground black pepper

serves 4

No one understands family cooking better than the Italians. This gorgeous soup is one of their classics – and it's a meal in itself. There are many versions of minestrone, according to which region of Italy a recipe comes from, but they are all good. This particular recipe uses smoked pancetta and bacon for a bit of extra flavour.

minestrone

Soak the beans overnight in at least 1.5 litres cold water to cover.

Drain, then put in a saucepan, cover with cold water and bring to the boil. Reduce the heat and simmer until almost tender (they will be cooked again, so don't let them get too soft). Do not add salt during this precooking, or you will have cannellini bullets. Drain and set aside.

Put the pancetta, garlic and parsley in a stockpot, heat gently and fry until the fat runs. Add the olive oil, heat briefly, then add the onion and cook gently until softened but not browned.

Add the potatoes, carrots, celery, tomatoes, salt and pepper. Add 3 litres water and heat until simmering. Cook over low heat for about 20 minutes. Add the rice and simmer for 10 minutes. Add the cabbage and reserved beans, bring to the boil and cook for 5 minutes, then add the peas and courgettes and cook for another 2–3 minutes until all the vegetables are tender. Remove and discard the parsley stalks, add salt and pepper to taste, then serve sprinkled with torn basil. Crusty Italian bread and a dish of freshly grated Parmesan are the perfect accompaniments.

note: Use canned or bottled beans if you prefer, but remember that they often have sugar and salt added, so keep that in mind when seasoning. They are already quite soft, so add them at the end and cook only until heated through.

200 g dried cannellini beans

250 g smoked pancetta or bacon, cut into cubes or strips

2 garlic cloves, crushed

2 large stalks of parsley, lightly crushed

1 tablespoon extra virgin olive oil

1 large onion, chopped

2 large potatoes, diced and rinsed

3 carrots, diced

2 celery stalks, sliced

3 tomatoes, halved, deseeded and chopped

200 g Italian risotto rice

1 small round cabbage, quartered, cored and sliced

250 g shelled peas, fresh or frozen

3 small courgettes, halved lengthways, halved again into quarters, then thickly sliced

sea salt and freshly ground black pepper

to serve

a handful of basil, torn

crusty bread

freshly grated Parmesan cheese

serves 6–8

From the land that brings us haggis, kippers, neeps and tatties comes its famous broth. Barley is traditionally used, but here it is substituted with brown rice. Although soy sauce is never used in traditional Scottish fare, it works well with the other flavours in this recipe. You could add some herbs as well, if you like. Thyme, in particular, is good with lamb.

scotch broth

Heat the oil in a large saucepan. Add the carrot, leek, celery stalks and leaves and cook over high heat for 5 minutes, stirring often. Add the lamb, stock, soy sauce, rice and 1 litre of water and bring to the boil.

Reduce the heat to low, cover with a tight-fitting lid and let the soup simmer for 1 hour. Season to taste with salt and pepper and serve with soft, buttered rolls on the side.

2 tablespoons light olive oil

1 carrot, diced

1 leek, diced

2 celery stalks, diced and leaves chopped

500 g stewing lamb, well trimmed of fat and cubed

500 ml chicken stock (page 41)

1 tablespoon light soy sauce

95 g brown rice

sea salt and freshly ground black pepper

serves 4

This is associated with the French tradition of serving onion soup at wedding parties in the early hours of the morning, as a restorative after a long night of celebrating. Here is a simplified version of the recipe, the sort of thing that's ideal when it's chilly outside, people are hungry inside and there's not much more than a few onions lurking about.

french onion soup

Put the butter and oil in a large saucepan and melt over medium heat. Add the onions and cook over low heat until soft, 15–20 minutes.

Add the garlic and flour and cook, stirring for about 1 minute. Add the stock, wine, bay leaf and thyme. Season with salt and pepper and bring to the boil. Boil for 1 minute, then lower the heat and simmer very gently for 20 minutes. Taste and adjust the seasoning. At this point, the soup will be cooked, but standing time will improve the flavour – at least 30 minutes.

Before serving, preheat the grill. Put the baguette slices on a baking sheet and brown under the grill until lightly toasted. Set aside.

To serve, ladle the soup into ovenproof bowls and top with a few toasted baguette rounds. Sprinkle the grated cheese over the top and cook under the grill until browned and bubbling. Serve immediately.

50 g unsalted butter

1 tablespoon extra virgin olive oil

3 large onions, about 1.3 kg, thinly sliced

2 garlic cloves, crushed

1 tablespoon plain flour

1 litre beef stock (page 40) or chicken stock (page 41)

600 ml dry white wine

1 fresh bay leaf

2 sprigs of thyme

coarse sea salt and freshly ground black pepper

to serve

1 baguette, or other white bread, sliced

about 180 g freshly grated Gruyère cheese

a baking sheet

serves 4–6

hot from the hob

beef and carrot casserole with cheesy dumplings · manhattan clam chowder · ratatouille · smoky sausage and bean casserole · creole gumbo · a bowl of red · parmesan and butter risotto · beef polpetti with tomato sauce and spaghetti · cock-a-leekie · sage pork chops with kale colcannon · steak and frites · best-ever beefburgers

Think of chilly, dark evenings and this is exactly the sort of warming food you'd want to eat. The feather-light dumplings nestling in the rich, savoury casserole will have everyone demanding more. A staple of British home cooking – with a touch of tangy Cheddar cheese in the dumplings to add an extra bite to the flavours.

beef and carrot casserole with cheesy dumplings

Heat the olive oil in a large casserole, add the garlic, onion and celery and sauté for 4 minutes. Transfer to a plate. Put the beef in the casserole, increase the heat and sauté for 5 minutes, stirring frequently. When the beef is cooked, return the onion mixture to the casserole. Add the stock, red wine, seasoning and bay leaves, bring to the boil, then reduce the heat to a gentle simmer. Cover and cook for 1½ hours.

To make the dumplings, place the flour and baking powder in a bowl and rub in the fat until it resembles breadcrumbs. Add the cheese, mixing it in with a knife. Add 75–100 ml water and use your hands to bring the mixture together and form a dough. Divide into 8 equal pieces and roll into balls.

Remove the casserole from the heat for about 5 minutes, then sift in the flour and stir to thicken the gravy. Return to the heat, add the carrots and stir until the casserole comes to a simmer. Place the dumplings on top, cover and cook for a further 20 minutes.

1 tablespoon extra virgin olive oil

2 garlic cloves, peeled and crushed

1 onion, diced

2 celery sticks, diced

800 g chuck steak, cut into cubes

400 ml beef stock (page 40)

200 ml red wine

2 bay leaves

25 g plain flour

4 carrots, cut into small chunks

sea salt and freshly ground black pepper

cheesy dumplings

200 g plain flour

1 teaspoon baking powder

75 g hard vegetable fat

75 g strong Cheddar cheese, grated

serves 4–6

Manhattan clam chowder is the tomato-based cousin of the creamy New England variety. Always buy your clams from a good fishmonger and check them to make sure they are in the best condition. Clams should have a fresh smell and their shells should look clean and unbroken.

manhattan clam chowder

Place the clams in a clean kitchen sink filled with very cold water and the salt. Leave for 30 minutes to draw out any impurities. Drain the clams and put them in a large, lidded pot. Add just enough water to cover by 5 cm. Cover with the lid and bring to the boil over high heat. Turn the heat down to low and cook for 1 minute. Remove the lid and, using a slotted spoon, set aside all the clams that have opened. Try reheating the ones that didn't open and discard any that still don't. Reserve the liquid and pass through a fine sieve. Leave the clams to cool slightly, then remove from their shells, roughly chop and set aside. Alternatively, you can leave the clams in their shells.

In a large saucepan, pan-fry the bacon until crisp. Pour off most of the fat, leaving 2 tablespoons. Add the onion, celery, garlic and carrot. Season and cook for 10 minutes. Add the potatoes, tomatoes, bay leaves, reserved clam liquid and clam juice. Bring to the boil and cook for a further 10 minutes. Add the clams and parsley and taste for additional seasoning. Serve with chunks of crusty bread.

40 small clams

a handful of salt

90 g dry-cured bacon, diced

1 large onion, finely diced

1 celery stick, finely diced

2 garlic cloves, finely chopped

1 large carrot, peeled and finely diced

2 medium potatoes, peeled and cut into 2-cm chunks

2 x 400-g tins peeled and chopped plum tomatoes

2 bay leaves

250 ml clam juice, or fish stock (page 43)

20 g fresh flat leaf parsley, chopped

sea salt and freshly ground pepper

serves 4

Meltingly delicious, ratatouille is wonderful served either as an accompaniment or as a main dish in its own right to be scooped up with crusty bread. For an authentic flavour, it is important to season each vegetable 'layer' individually. Cutting the vegetables into medium-large pieces about 3–4 cm, helps to keep them separate.

ratatouille

Heat 3 tablespoons of the oil in a large casserole with a lid. Cook the aubergine pieces over medium heat, 5 minutes each side. Add the onions and cook until soft, another 3–5 minutes. Salt lightly.

Add all the peppers and cook for 5–8 minutes more, stirring often. Turn up the heat to keep the sizzling sound going, but take care not to let it burn. Salt lightly.

Add 1 more tablespoon of the oil and the courgettes. Mix well and cook for about 5 minutes more, stirring occasionally. Salt lightly.

Add the garlic and cook for 1 minute. Add 1 more tablespoon of the oil if necessary, and the tomatoes and basil and stir well. Salt lightly. Cook for 5 minutes, then cover, lower the heat and simmer gently for 30 minutes, checking from time to time.

Remove from the heat. This is best served at room temperature, but it still tastes nice hot. The longer you let it stand, the richer it tastes. Stir in extra basil and garlic just before serving.

1 kg aubergines, cut into pieces

extra virgin olive oil (see method)

2 medium onions, coarsely chopped

2 red peppers, halved, deseeded and cut into pieces

2 yellow peppers, halved, deseeded and cut into pieces

1 green pepper, halved, deseeded and cut into pieces

6 smallish courgettes, about 750 g, halved lengthways and sliced

4 garlic cloves, crushed

6 medium tomatoes, halved, deseeded and chopped

a small bunch of basil, coarsely chopped

coarse sea salt

to serve

a few basil leaves, finely sliced

1 garlic clove, crushed

serves 4–6

A mixture of onions, carrots and celery sautéed in olive oil forms the base of a hearty stew with sausages and beans. This casserole is easy to prepare and doesn't take hours to cook – ideal if you want to put a nourishing meal on the table without a long hungry wait.

smoky sausage and bean casserole

Heat the oil in a heavy-based casserole or saucepan over high heat. Add the sausages in two batches and cook them for 4–5 minutes, turning often until cooked and an even brown on all sides. Remove them from the casserole and set aside.

Add the garlic, leek, carrot and celery and cook for 5 minutes, stirring often. Add the tomatoes, paprika, maple syrup, thyme, beans and 500 ml water and return the sausages to the pan.

Bring to the boil, then reduce the heat to medium and simmer for 40–45 minutes, until the sauce has thickened.

Put a slice of toasted sourdough bread on each serving plate, spoon the casserole over the top and serve.

variation: Try replacing the sausages with 500 g pork neck fillet cut into 2–3-cm pieces. Cook the pork in batches for 4–5 minutes each batch, turning often so each piece is evenly browned. Return all the pork to the pan, as you would the sausages, and simmer for 45–50 minutes until the pork is tender.

1 tablespoon light olive oil

12 chipolata sausages

1 garlic clove, chopped

1 leek, thinly sliced

1 carrot, diced

1 celery stalk, diced

400 g canned chopped tomatoes

1 teaspoon Spanish smoked paprika

2 tablespoons maple syrup

2 sprigs of fresh thyme

400 g canned cannellini beans, drained and rinsed

to serve
toasted sourdough bread

a heavy-based casserole or saucepan

serves 4

Gumbos are the classic Creole stews, thick and bubbling with flavours.
This one features shellfish but the dish is also often made with chicken
or a variety of meats. Serve with a mound of steamed white rice.

creole gumbo

Pour 500 ml lightly salted water into a large saucepan and bring to the boil. Press in the watercress, parsley, spinach, spring onions and chard or beet greens. Cover and cook until just tender, about 5 minutes. Strain, reserving the cooking water. Chop the greens and set aside.

To make the stock, peel the prawns and put the shells and heads, if any, into a large saucepan or casserole dish. Add the reserved cooking water, stock or water, thyme, marjoram, bay leaves and allspice. Simmer for 15 minutes then strain into a saucepan, return to the boil, reduce the heat and keep warm.

Heat the butter or oil in a large casserole dish, add the flour and fry gently until the flour turns a hazelnut colour, about 10 minutes: do not let the butter burn. Add the garlic, onion and cayenne pepper and sauté for 2 minutes. Add the crab claws, then the reserved hot stock and the sausage, if using. Bring to the boil.

Add the clams, return to the boil, then simmer, covered, for about 15 minutes or until the clams open. Meanwhile, to prepare the okra, trim carefully around the stalk end, without cutting into the middle.

As the clams open, remove them to a plate with a slotted spoon. This will stop them overcooking. Discard any that remain closed. Add the okra to the pan. Return the reserved chopped greens to the casserole and bring to the boil. Add a dash of Tabasco sauce.

Share the seafood, okra and greens between 4 large bowls, ladle the stock over the top, then serve with steamed white rice.

1 bunch of watercress, washed and trimmed

1 bunch of parsley, washed and trimmed

1 bunch of spinach, washed and trimmed

10 spring onions, green ends only

1 bunch of chard or beet greens, washed and trimmed

500 g uncooked, unpeeled prawns

1 litre chicken stock (page 41) or water

1 sprig of thyme

1 sprig of marjoram

2 bay leaves

5 whole allspice berries

1½ tablespoons butter or peanut oil

2 tablespoons plain flour

2 garlic cloves, crushed

1 onion, chopped

½ teaspoon cayenne pepper

4 crab claws, preferably uncooked

250 g Creole smoked garlic sausage (andouille) or Polish sausage, cut into 1-cm slices (optional)

2–3 dozen clams and/or mussels, well scrubbed and debearded if necessary

8–12 medium okra

1 teaspoon Tabasco sauce

serves 4

Chunks of tender steak and puréed dried chillies make this mouth-watering chilli something special. A bowlful goes down well on any occasion from a family meal to a more formal supper party.

a bowl of red

Put the beef in a medium bowl, pour the beer over and leave to marinate for 30 minutes. Drain, reserving the liquid and pat the beef dry with kitchen paper. Toast the chillies for 30 seconds in a dry sauté pan then pour boiling water over and soak for 15 minutes or until soft. Drain and put in a food processor with the beer. Purée until fine and set aside.

In a large saucepan, heat 2 tablespoons of the olive oil. Season the meat and sear in batches until evenly browned. Remove from the pan and set aside. Add the remaining olive oil and sauté the onions and garlic for 5 minutes. Put the meat back in the pan and pour the chilli mixture over.

Purée the tomatoes in the food processor and add to the pan. Add the cider vinegar, brown sugar, paprika, chilli powder and cumin, and season. Cook, partially covered with a lid, for 1 hour over low heat or until the meat is very tender. Add the beans in the last 5 minutes of cooking to warm through. Serve in small bowls with your choice of accompaniments, which could include steamed white rice, chopped red onion or coriander.

1 kg braising steak, cut into 4-cm chunks

1 bottle beer

4 ancho chillies, stemmed and deseeded

6 tablespoons extra virgin olive oil

2 large onions, roughly chopped

6 garlic cloves, finely chopped

2 x 400-g tins whole, peeled plum tomatoes

75 ml cider vinegar

60 g brown sugar

1 tablespoon Spanish paprika (preferably pimentón)

1 tablespoon mild chilli powder

3 tablespoons cumin seeds, toasted and ground

400-g tin kidney, borlotti or pinto beans, drained and rinsed

sea salt and freshly ground black pepper

serves 4–6

When you have nothing except risotto rice in the cupboard, and a chunk of Parmesan and some butter in the refrigerator, yet feel the need for comfort and luxury, this is the risotto for you. It is pale, golden, smooth and creamy and relies totally on the quality of these few ingredients. Real sweet, nutty Parmigiano Reggiano is best of all.

parmesan and butter risotto

Put the stock in a saucepan and keep it at a gentle simmer. Melt half the butter in a large, heavy saucepan and add the onion. Cook gently for 10 minutes until the onion is soft, golden and translucent but not browned. Add the rice and stir until well coated with the butter and heated through. Pour in the wine and boil hard until it has reduced and almost disappeared. This will remove the taste of alcohol.

Begin adding the stock, a large ladle at a time, stirring gently until each ladle has been almost absorbed by the rice. The risotto should be kept at a bare simmer throughout cooking, so don't let the rice dry out – add more stock as necessary. Continue until the rice is tender and creamy, but the grains still firm. (This should take 15–20 minutes depending on the type of rice used – check the packet instructions.)

Taste and season well with salt and pepper, then stir in the remaining butter and all the Parmesan. Cover and let rest for a couple of minutes so the risotto can relax and the cheese melt, then serve immediately. You may like to add a little more stock just before serving, but don't let the risotto wait around too long or the rice will turn mushy.

about 1.5 litres hot chicken stock (page 41) or vegetable stock (page 43)

150 g unsalted butter

1 onion, finely chopped

500 g risotto rice, preferably carnaroli

150 ml dry white wine

100 g freshly grated Parmesan cheese

sea salt and freshly ground black pepper

serves 4–6

Italian mothers often put polpetti – meatballs – on the menu when they need to provide a filling and economical meal. In this recipe, the addition of breadcrumbs is not just a thrifty measure. The bread lightens the polpetti and also absorbs much more of the sauce and the flavoursome oil released by the meat. Serve on Sunday night with a glass of Chianti.

beef polpetti with tomato sauce and spaghetti

Preheat the oven to 200°C (400°F) Gas 6.

To make the tomato sauce, put the olive oil, garlic, onion, tomatoes and basil in a saucepan, season well and bring to the boil. Reduce the heat and simmer gently for at least 40 minutes while you prepare the meatballs.

To make the meatballs, put the minced beef, breadcrumbs, eggs, Parmesan, parsley and olive oil in a large mixing bowl, season and combine with your hands. Shape the mixture into roughly 20 walnut-sized balls and put in a single layer on a baking sheet covered with foil. Roast in the oven for 10 minutes, turn, then roast for a further 6–7 minutes.

Put a saucepan of salted water on to boil for the spaghetti. When it comes to the boil, drop in the spaghetti and cook according to the instructions on the packet until al dente. Drain, return to the pan and add the tomato sauce and meatballs. Stir very gently so as not to break up the meatballs. Take out the onion wedges if you prefer. Transfer to bowls and sprinkle with basil and grated Parmesan to serve.

300–400 g spaghetti
sea salt and freshly ground black pepper

tomato sauce

4 tablespoons extra virgin olive oil

3 cloves garlic, peeled and thinly sliced

1 large onion, cut into wedges

2 x 400-g tins chopped plum tomatoes

20 g fresh basil, plus extra to serve

meatballs

250 g beef mince

100 g fresh white breadcrumbs

2 eggs

25 g freshly grated Parmesan cheese, plus extra to serve

4 tablespoons chopped fresh parsley

3 tablespoons extra virgin olive oil

serves 4

Cock-a-leekie is a Scottish classic, consisting mainly of chicken wings, giblets and barley – an easy, economical 'big soup' meal. In the past, in the small stone crofts, a whole chicken and its broth would bubble deliciously in a cauldron hung in the open fireplace. Prunes add extra sweetness, but a little brown sugar could do instead.

cock-a-leekie

Put the wings, giblets, beef, whites of the leeks, thyme, parsley stalks, pearl barley and onions in a large saucepan and add the boiling water.

Bring to the boil, reduce the heat, cover and simmer over medium heat for 50–60 minutes. For the last 15–20 minutes, add the potatoes, prunes and finely shredded green parts of the leeks and cook until the potatoes are done.

Using tongs and a slotted spoon, carefully take the beef out of the saucepan and put it on a plate. Cut the beef into 4 pieces and return them to the soup. Taste and adjust the seasoning.

Ladle the soup into large bowls, sprinkle with the chopped parsley and serve accompanied by crusty bread rolls.

variation: If you prefer, you may omit the beef altogether, but adjust the seasonings carefully to balance the flavours.

500 g large chicken wings

250 g chicken giblets, excluding liver, or extra wings

250 g stewing beef

750 g leeks, whites cut into 1.5-cm slices, green parts finely shredded

a small bunch of fresh thyme, tied with string

a few fresh parsley stalks, plus 4 tablespoons chopped leaves, to serve

2 tablespoons pearl barley

2 onions, quartered

2 litres boiling water

2 large potatoes, quartered

12 stoned prunes or 1 tablespoon brown sugar

sea salt and freshly ground black pepper

serves 4

Easy to prepare, these sage-crumbed pork chops are served with Irish-style colcannon. This is comfort food at its best – creamy mashed potato traditionally combined with cooked cabbage. Here, the recipe uses kale, a close relative of the cabbage. Kale is at its best in colder weather, so this dish is a good choice for chilly autumn days.

sage pork chops with kale colcannon

Put the plain flour on a flat plate. Mix the eggs and Worcestershire sauce in a bowl and, in a separate bowl, combine the sage, breadcrumbs and Parmesan. Press a pork chop into the flour, coating the meat evenly, then dip it in the egg mixture, then press firmly to coat in the crumb mix. Repeat this process with all 4 pork chops. Transfer them to a plate and keep refrigerated until needed.

To make the colcannon, cook the kale in a large saucepan of boiling water for 5 minutes. Drain well, chop finely and set aside.

Put the 2 tablespoons of butter in a frying pan over medium heat. Add the bacon and cook for 5 minutes, stirring occasionally until the bacon turns golden. Add the spring onions and cook for a further 2 minutes. Stir in the kale and remove the pan from the heat.

Put the potatoes in a large saucepan and cover with cold water. Bring to the boil and cook for 20 minutes, until soft when pierced with a skewer but not breaking apart. Drain the potatoes well and return them to the pan. Add the butter and mash well. Beat with a wooden spoon until smooth. Stir the kale mixture into the potatoes, cover and keep warm while cooking the pork.

Heat the vegetable oil in a large frying pan over medium heat. When hot, add the pork chops and cook for 6–7 minutes, so they gently sizzle in the oil and a golden crust forms. Turn over the pork chops and cook for 5 minutes on the other side. Serve with a portion of the kale colcannon.

60 g plain flour

3 eggs

2 tablespoons Worcestershire sauce

4–6 fresh sage leaves, finely chopped

100 g fresh breadcrumbs

100 g Parmesan cheese, finely grated

4 pork chops

60 ml vegetable oil

kale colcannon

500 g curly kale

2 tablespoons butter

2 rashers of bacon, thinly sliced

6–8 spring onions, thinly sliced

4 large potatoes, quartered

125 g butter, cut into cubes

serves 4

The shallot butter is a fancy flourish that gives this standard 'pub grub'
a real home-cooked taste. You could also serve the steaks with tarragon-
flavoured béarnaise sauce (page 154) or simply Dijon mustard.

steak and frites

To make the shallot butter, put about 25 g of the butter in a saucepan and melt over low heat. Add the shallots and cook until softened. Add the wine, bring to the boil and cook until syrupy and the wine has almost evaporated. Set aside to cool.

Put the cooled shallots, remaining butter, tarragon, parsley, salt and pepper in a small food processor and blend briefly. Transfer the mixture to a piece of baking parchment and shape into a log. Roll up and chill until firm.

To prepare the frites, peel the potatoes and cut into 5 mm slices. Cut the slices into 5 mm strips. Put into a bowl of iced water for 5 minutes. Drain and pat dry with kitchen paper.

Fill a large saucepan one-third full with the oil, or if using a deep-fryer to the manufacturer's recommended level. Heat the oil to 190°C (375°F) or until a cube of bread will brown in 30 seconds. Working in batches, put 2 large handfuls of potato strips into the frying basket, lower carefully into the oil and fry for about 4 minutes.

Remove and drain on kitchen paper. Skim any debris off the oil, heat to the same temperature again, then fry the strips for a second time, about 2 minutes. Remove, drain on kitchen paper, then sprinkle with salt. Keep hot in the oven until ready to serve.

To cook the steaks, rub oil on both sides. Heat a ridged stove-top grill pan, add the steaks and cook for 1½–2 minutes on each side. This produces a rare steak. For medium-rare steaks, cook again on both sides for 2–3 minutes. Remove from the pan, season, then serve with rounds of the butter and the frites.

4 sirloin or rib eye steaks, about 300 g each, 3 cm thick

1 tablespoon sunflower oil

shallot butter

100 g unsalted butter, softened

2 shallots, finely chopped

150 ml red wine

a large sprig of tarragon

several sprigs of flat leaf parsley

1 teaspoon coarse sea salt

½ teaspoon coarsely ground black pepper

frites

500 g floury potatoes (for baking and frying)

sunflower oil, for frying

sea salt, to serve

a large saucepan with frying basket, or electric deep-fryer

serves 4

There are many burger recipes and everyone has his or her favourite –
this one is very good. If you have children, they will probably enjoy
helping you to shape the burger mix. Serve in a bun with onions, pickles
and sauce, and offer a simple salad of tomatoes, lettuce and olives.

best-ever beefburgers

Put the minced steak and pork into a bowl and
add the anchovies, breadcrumbs, thyme,
mustard, beaten egg, salt and pepper, working it
with your hands to make a nice, sticky mixture.

Shape into 6 burgers and chill for 1 hour. Cook
on a preheated barbecue or in a lightly oiled
frying pan for about 4 minutes on each side.
Remove from the heat and let rest for 5 minutes.
Serve in a bun, with fried onions, dill pickles and
the tomato, lettuce and olive salad, if using.

note: To make the burger mince, ask your
butcher to put the beef and pork through a meat
mincer. Alternatively, put it into a food processor
and pulse briefly to make a slightly coarse mince.

750 g sirloin steak, minced (see note)

50 g skinless pork belly,
minced (see note)

8 anchovy fillets in oil, drained and finely
chopped

50 g fresh white breadcrumbs

2 tablespoons chopped fresh thyme

1 tablespoon wholegrain mustard

1 large egg, lightly beaten

sea salt and freshly ground black pepper

to serve

hamburger buns

fried onions

dill pickles (gherkins)

tomato, lettuce and olive salad (optional)

serves 6

fresh from the oven

Macaroni cheese, brown and bubbling on top, is the perfect 'instant'
food. Here, this simple family standby is given a touch of sophistication
with Beaufort cheese, which has a more subtle flavour than the usual
Cheddar. It makes a substantial meal in itself but it also works
particularly well served as an accompaniment to beef stews.

macaroni gratin

Cook the macaroni in plenty of boiling, salted
water according to the instructions on the
packet. Drain, rinse well with boiling water and
return to the empty saucepan.

Heat the milk in a saucepan and stir in the crème
fraîche. Melt the butter in a second saucepan
over medium-high heat. Stir in the flour and
cook, stirring constantly for 3 minutes. Pour
in the milk mixture and stir constantly until the
mixture thickens. Season with salt and pepper.

Stir the milk mixture into the macaroni and taste,
adding salt and pepper if necessary. Transfer
to the baking dish and sprinkle with the cheese.
Cook under a preheated grill until bubbling and
browned, 10–15 minutes. Serve hot.

note: Beaufort is an alpine cheese, similar to
Gruyère, but with a slightly sweeter, more
pronounced nutty flavour. It is becoming more
widely available in supermarkets, but if you
cannot find it, Emmental, Cantal or any firm,
Cheddar-like cheese will do. The taste will be
entirely different, of course.

300 g thin macaroni

500 ml milk

3 tablespoons crème fraîche

60 g unsalted butter

4 tablespoons plain flour

coarse sea salt and freshly
ground black pepper

200 g finely grated Beaufort
cheese (see note)

*a baking dish, 30 cm long,
greased with butter*

serves 6

This recipe is based on that all-time classic, the Neapolitan pizza. It should please busy working mothers because it cheats – a little – by using ready-made pizza dough. But the richly flavoured topping is authentic and made with fresh ingredients.

pizza margherita

Preheat the oven to 220°C (425°F) Gas 7.

To make the pizzaiola sauce, heat the oil in a shallow pan until it is almost smoking hot. Carefully add the garlic, oregano and tomatoes (they will sputter, so stand back) and cook on high heat for 5–8 minutes. Season to taste. Press the sauce through a food mill into a bowl to remove the tomato seeds and skin.

Lightly squeeze any excess moisture out of the mozzarella, then roughly slice it.

Put the pizza base on the baking sheet. Spread the pizzaiola sauce over the dough with the back of a spoon, leaving a 1-cm rim around the edge. Scatter with the tomatoes and season.

Put in the heated oven and bake for 5 minutes, then remove from the oven and scatter the mozzarella over the tomatoes. Return the pizza to the oven and bake for a further 15 minutes or until the crust is golden and the cheese melted but still white. Remove from the oven, scatter with the basil leaves and drizzle with olive oil. Eat immediately.

note: These quantities make about 400 ml of sauce. Keep the leftovers refrigerated in a tightly sealed container to use with pasta.

50–75 g buffalo mozzarella or cow's milk mozzarella (fior di latte)

1 large ready-made pizza dough base

3–4 tablespoons pizzaiola sauce
(see below)

200 g very ripe cherry tomatoes, halved

a good handful of fresh basil leaves

extra virgin olive oil, to drizzle

sea salt and freshly ground black pepper

pizzaiola sauce (see note)

8 tablespoons olive oil

2 garlic cloves, chopped

1 teaspoon dried oregano

800 g fresh tomatoes, halved and cored

a rimless baking sheet

makes 1 medium-crust pizza, 25–35 cm

Who doesn't have nostalgic longings for meat loaf? Not school stodge, of course, but the utterly delicious home-baked variety. Here meat loaf is served with two tomato sauces, one spicy for adventurous eaters.

meat loaf with two sauces

Preheat the oven to 170°C (325°F) Gas 3.

Line the loaf tin with the Parma ham, leaving some aside to cover the top of the finished loaf.

Put the chicken livers in a bowl with the pork and turkey, add the onion, eggs, bay leaves and parsley, season and mix well. This is best done with your hands.

Fill the prepared tin with the meat, flatten out the top and cover with the remaining ham. Cover with foil and bake in the oven for 1 hour 15 minutes. Remove and let stand for 10 minutes. Drain off any juice into a jug, then turn out the meat loaf onto a deep plate.

To make the tomato sauce, heat the oil and sauté the onion gently for 5 minutes. Add the garlic and cook for a further 5 minutes. Add the tomatoes and reserved meat juices, season and simmer gently for 30 minutes, stirring frequently.

To make the spiced tomato sauce, pour half of the tomato sauce mixture into another pan, add the chopped chilli and simmer for 10 minutes. Serve both sauces with the meat loaf.

12 slices Parma ham

200 g chicken livers, chopped

400 g lean pork, diced

300 g minced turkey or chicken

1 red onion, diced

2 eggs, beaten

3 bay leaves, torn

a bunch of flat leaf parsley, chopped

sea salt and freshly ground black pepper

tomato sauce and spiced tomato sauce

3 tablespoons olive oil

1 onion, diced

2 garlic cloves, crushed

2 x 400-g cans chopped tomatoes

1 red chilli, chopped

a 1-kg loaf tin

serves 6

For many people, the smell of roasting chicken conjures up childhood memories of a cosy Sunday at home. It's always worth cooking a larger bird than you need because the leftovers can be used in a pilaf or to make sandwiches. You can also use the carcass to make stock and freeze it. Three meals for the price of one bird!

roast chicken with lemon, thyme and potato stuffing

Preheat the oven to 180°C (350°F) Gas 4. Lightly oil a roasting tin.

Take the chicken and carefully slide the lemon slices and bay leaves between the skin and the breast meat.

To make the stuffing, put the garlic, onion, thyme, potato and sausagemeat in a large bowl. Add the lemon zest and juice, season and mix well. Cut any excess fat from the cavity of the chicken, then stuff the bird.

Weigh your chicken to work out the cooking time: you should allow 20 minutes per 500 g, plus 20 minutes extra. Put the chicken in the prepared roasting tin and lay the bacon rashers over the breast. Put in the hot oven and cook for the calculated time. When the chicken is ready, remove it from the roasting tin and keep warm.

Now make the gravy. Add the flour to the tin and stir with a wooden spoon to combine with the fat and juices. Slowly pour in the chicken stock, stirring continuously to prevent lumps forming. Put the roasting tin directly on the heat and bring to the boil. When the mixture has thickened, remove it from the heat and season well. If you like a very smooth gravy, press it through a sieve with the back of a spoon.

1 medium free-range chicken

1 unwaxed lemon, thinly sliced

4 bay leaves

4 bacon rashers

sea salt and freshly ground black pepper

stuffing

2 garlic cloves, peeled and crushed

1 onion, finely diced

leaves from 4 sprigs of fresh thyme

1 large potato, coarsely grated

300 g sausagemeat

zest and juice of 1 unwaxed lemon

gravy

25 g plain flour

500 ml chicken stock (page 41)

serves 4

Simple, tasty and low-cost – the humble toad-in-the-hole makes a great
midweek supper dish. This takes little time to prepare and will be
popular with all the family. You can serve it with any vegetables you like,
but mashed potato and your favourite gravy are particularly good.

sausage and bacon toad-in-the-hole

Preheat the oven to 220°C (425°F) Gas 7.

Put the flour in a mixing bowl and make a well in
the centre. Whisk the eggs, milk, seasoning and
150 ml water together and pour into the well.
Stir carefully with a wooden spoon until you have
a smooth batter. Leave to rest for 30 minutes.

Grease a large roasting tin or 4–6 individual
dishes and place in the oven.

Wrap the bacon around the sausages and place
in the hot roasting tin or dishes. Add the onion,
then pour in the batter. Return to the oven and
bake for 30 minutes without opening the door.
The batter should be light and well risen.

175 g flour

2 eggs

150 ml milk

8 streaky bacon rashers

800 g sausages

2 red onions, cut into wedges

sea salt and freshly ground black pepper

serves 4–6

Nothing beats a steaming, creamy fish pie – light but satisfying. The hint of mustard and the addition of hard-boiled eggs lift this from an ordinary supper dish to a fantastic winner of a pie. If you use smoked haddock, try to buy the pale yellow (undyed) fish.

traditional fish pie

Preheat the oven to 200°C (400°F) Gas 6.

Put the milk in a wide saucepan, heat just to boiling point, then add the fish. Turn off the heat and leave the fish to poach until opaque – do not over-cook.

Meanwhile, melt 125 g of the butter in another saucepan, then stir in the mustard and flour. Remove from the heat and strain the poaching liquid into the pan.

Arrange the fish and eggs in a shallow pie dish or casserole.

Return the pan to the heat and, whisking vigorously to smooth out any lumps, bring the mixture to the boil. Season to taste. (Take care: if you are using smoked fish, it may be salty enough.) Pour the sauce into the casserole and mix carefully with the fish and eggs.

Cook the potatoes in boiling salted water until soft, then drain. Return to the pan. Melt the remaining 150 g butter in a small saucepan. Reserve 4 tablespoons of this butter and stir the remainder into the potatoes. Mash well and season. Spoon the mixture carefully over the sauced fish, brush with the reserved butter and transfer to the oven. Cook for 20 minutes, or until nicely browned.

note: If you can't find smoked haddock, you can sprinkle 125 g smoked salmon, finely sliced, over the poached fresh haddock just before adding the sauce.

500 ml milk

750 g smoked or fresh haddock, skinned

275 g unsalted butter

1 tablespoon English mustard powder

4 tablespoons plain flour

2 hard-boiled eggs, peeled and quartered

1 kg floury potatoes

sea salt and freshly ground black pepper

serves 4

The traditional recipe calls for leftover cooked beef, so if you had a Sunday roast, this pie is perfect for Monday supper. Otherwise, mince that has been well seasoned and cooked in a splash of wine comes a close second. Serve with a fruity red wine.

cottage pie

Preheat the oven to 200°C (400°F) Gas 6.

To make the mashed potato, put the potatoes and bay leaf in a saucepan of cold water. Bring to the boil, add salt and cook until tender. Drain.

Put the potatoes in a large bowl and mash coarsely with a wooden spoon. Using an electric whisk, gradually add the milk and butter, beating until the mixture is smooth. Add salt and whisk well. If the potatoes are very dry, add more milk. Taste, then add more butter and/or salt as necessary and set aside.

Heat the butter in a frying pan, add the onions and cook over high heat until just brown, 3–5 minutes. Add the garlic, beef and bacon and cook until almost completely browned. Add the wine and cook until almost evaporated. Stir in the parsley, thyme leaves and tomato purée. Season to taste.

Spread the beef mixture over the baking dish and level with a spoon. Spread with the potatoes. Sprinkle with the cheese and bake in the oven until golden, about 25–30 minutes.

30 g unsalted butter or 2 tablespoons sunflower oil

2 onions, chopped

2 garlic cloves

750 g beef mince

70 g bacon, finely chopped

125 ml dry white wine

a handful of fresh flat leaf parsley, chopped

a fresh thyme sprig, leaves stripped

2 tablespoons tomato purée

50 g freshly grated Cheddar cheese

sea salt and freshly ground black pepper

potato topping

2 kg potatoes

1 bay leaf

250 ml hot milk

100 g unsalted butter, cubed

sea salt

a baking dish, about 30 cm long

serves 4–6

What exactly is an heirloom tomato? Opinions vary and include classification based on the age of the seed. One explanation is that an heirloom is a variety that has been nurtured and handed down from generation to generation within a family. You will find heirlooms in farmers' markets. Choose a variety that stays fairly firm when cooked.

upside-down heirloom tomato tart

Preheat the oven to 220°C (425°F) Gas 7.

Put the oil, capers and rosemary in a heatproof non-stick frying pan. Put over high heat and when the capers start to sizzle add the tomatoes, firmly pressing them down in a single layer in the pan. Cook for 3–4 minutes to allow the tomatoes to sizzle and soften.

Place the sheet of pastry over the tomatoes, folding in the corners, being careful not to press down on the tomatoes. Transfer the pan to the preheated oven and cook for 18–20 minutes, until the pastry is puffed and golden. Remove the pan from the oven and let the tart rest for a couple of minutes.

Place a serving plate that is larger than the frying pan upside-down on top of the pan and quickly flip the pan over so the tart falls onto the plate. Sprinkle with cracked black pepper and a drizzle of olive oil and cut into 4 wedges to serve.

variation: Make a roasted tomato sauce using prime summer tomatoes. Cut 6 medium tomatoes in half and place them on a baking sheet, cut side up, with 1 sliced red onion, 3 sliced garlic cloves, 2 tablespoons olive oil and ½ teaspoon each of sea salt and white sugar sprinkled over. Bake in a preheated oven at 170°C (325°F) Gas 3 for 1½ hours. Remove from the oven and process in a food processor with 3–4 fresh basil leaves, until you have a chunky sauce. Serve with pasta of your choice.

2 tablespoons light olive oil

2 teaspoons small capers, rinsed if salted

10–12 fresh rosemary needles

3 ripe tomatoes, thickly sliced

375-g sheet ready-rolled puff pastry, defrosted if frozen

cracked black pepper

extra virgin olive oil, for drizzling

a non-stick, heatproof frying pan 20–23 cm diameter

serves 4, as a starter

This classic tart is the forerunner of many versions of quiche. Made with light, crumbly shortcrust pastry filled with the best ingredients, this simplest of dishes is food fit for the gods – and a family favourite, of course. A touch of grated Gruyère adds interest to the flavour.

quiche lorraine

Preheat the oven to 200°C (400°F) Gas 6.

To make the pastry, sift the flour and salt into a large bowl. Rub in the lard and butter with your fingers until the mixture looks like breadcrumbs. Lightly mix in the water with a knife.

Roll out the pastry thinly on a lightly floured work surface and press it into the tart tin. Prick the base, and chill or freeze for 15 minutes. Then line the base with foil or parchment, fill with baking beans and bake blind in the oven for 10–12 minutes.

Remove the pastry from the oven and remove the foil and baking beans. Brush the pastry with a little beaten egg and return to the oven for another 5–10 minutes.

Heat a non-stick frying pan and fry the bacon or pancetta until brown and crisp, then drain on kitchen paper. Scatter over the pastry base.

Put the eggs and cream or crème fraîche into a bowl, beat well, and season with salt, pepper and nutmeg to taste. Carefully pour the mixture over the bacon and sprinkle with the Gruyère.

Bake for 25 minutes or until just set and golden brown. Serve warm or at room temperature.

200 g bacon lardons or cubed pancetta

5 medium eggs

200 ml double cream or crème fraîche

freshly grated nutmeg, to taste

50 g Gruyère cheese, grated

sea salt and freshly ground black pepper

shortcrust pastry

250 g plain flour

a pinch of salt

50 g lard or white cooking fat, chilled and diced

75 g unsalted butter, chilled and cubed

2–3 tablespoons chilled water

a little beaten egg

a tart tin, 23 cm diameter

baking beans

serves 4–6

This will be a popular choice for autumn meals. No one needs persuading to eat chicken pie – and it celebrates the season with fresh-grown leeks, at their very best in the cooler weather.

tarragon, chicken and leek pot pie

Preheat the oven to 180°C (350°F) Gas 4.

Heat half the butter in a frying pan over high heat. When it sizzles, cook the chicken in two batches for 2–3 minutes, turning often to brown the pieces all over. Transfer to a bowl.

Add the remaining butter to the pan and cook the leeks over medium heat for 2 minutes. Cover with a lid, reduce the heat, and cook for 2–3 minutes, until really softened.

Return the chicken to the pan and increase the heat to high. Sprinkle the flour into the pan and cook for 2 minutes, stirring constantly to coat the chicken and leeks. Gradually add the stock, stirring all the time. Bring to the boil, then stir in the cream, tarragon and parsley. Season well. Reduce the heat and simmer until thickened, about 1 minute. Remove from the heat and let cool. Spoon into an ovenproof pie dish.

To make the pastry, put the flour, butter and a pinch of salt in a food processor and process for a few seconds. With the motor running, add the sour cream, half the beaten egg and 1–2 tablespoons cold water, until the dough comes together. Roll into a ball, wrap in clingfilm and refrigerate for 30 minutes.

Place the dough between two pieces of greaseproof paper and roll out to a thickness of 0.5 cm. Fold the dough over the top of the pie, leaving the edges to overhang. Cut slits in the top of the pie and press gently around the edges with a fork. Brush the remaining beaten egg over the top. Put the pie dish on a baking sheet and cook in the preheated oven for 30 minutes, until the pastry is golden.

3 tablespoons butter

750 g organic chicken thigh fillets, cut into bite-sized pieces

4 medium leeks (white parts only), thickly sliced

3 tablespoons plain flour

250 ml chicken stock (page 41)

125 ml single cream

2 tablespoons finely chopped fresh tarragon

2 tablespoons roughly chopped flat leaf parsley

sea salt and freshly ground black pepper

pastry

185 g plain flour

2 tablespoons butter

2 tablespoons sour cream

1 egg, lightly beaten

1.5-litre ovenproof pie dish

serves 4

You can assemble this the day before, refrigerate it, put in the oven at the last moment and then wait for the family's applause! It's fine to vary the type of cheese, as long as it is a soft one.

ricotta, basil and cherry tomato cannelloni

Preheat the oven to 220°C (425°F) Gas 7.

Cut 250 g of the whole cherry tomatoes in half and set aside for the top.

Heat the oil in a frying pan, add the uncut tomatoes (they will splutter a little) and cover tightly. Cook over high heat, shaking the pan occasionally, for 5 minutes until the tomatoes start to break down. Uncover and stir in the oregano, sugar, salt and pepper. Set aside.

Soften the cheese in a bowl and beat in the pesto. Put all the sheets of lasagne on a work surface and spread the cheese mixture evenly over them. Put 2 tomato slices on each sheet, season well and roll up from the narrow side like a Swiss roll. Spoon half the tomato sauce in the bottom of the baking dish. Put the pasta rolls on top of the sauce, then spoon over the remaining sauce. Dot with the reserved cherry tomato halves and cover with foil.

Bake in the preheated oven for 25–30 minutes. Uncover, sprinkle with the Parmesan and bake or grill for a further 10 minutes until beginning to brown. Remove from the oven and let stand for 10 minutes before serving.

Top with basil and serve with a crisp green salad.

note: If using dried lasagne sheets, cook in boiling salted water according to the packet instructions. Carefully lift them out of the water and drain through a colander. Transfer to a bowl of cold water. Lift out and drain each sheet before spreading with the cheese mixture.

750 g ripe cherry tomatoes, whole, plus 350 g vine-ripened tomatoes, thinly sliced (you need 24 slices)

5 tablespoons extra virgin olive oil

2 teaspoons dried oregano

2 teaspoons sugar

300 g ricotta cheese

6 tablespoons fresh pesto (page 164)

12 sheets of fresh lasagne (see note)

3 tablespoons freshly grated Parmesan cheese

a handful of basil leaves

sea salt and freshly ground black pepper

green salad, to serve

a baking dish, 20 x 25 cm, lightly oiled

serves 4

These lip-smackingly good ribs are basted and then left in a full-flavoured marinade overnight. Teenagers love them as finger-food! It is important to use fresh sweetcorn for the salsa and shuck it just before cooking. So don't buy cobs smothered with plastic packaging. Instead, look for summer-ripened ones still in their silky skins.

sticky spare ribs with fresh sweetcorn salsa

To make the marinade, put the maple syrup, sugar, vinegar, fish sauce, garlic and chillies in a saucepan and bring to the boil, stirring constantly, until the sugar has dissolved. Simmer for 10 minutes until the mixture has thickened. Remove from the heat and let cool. Put the ribs in a large flat dish with the marinade, cover and refrigerate overnight, turning the ribs often.

Preheat the oven to 200°C (400°F) Gas 6.

To make the salsa, heat 1 tablespoon of the olive oil in a frying pan over high heat. Add the sweetcorn and cook for 4–5 minutes, stirring often, until the kernels start to turn golden. Add the onion and chilli and stir for 1 minute to just soften the onions a little. Remove from the heat and let cool. Stir in the remaining olive oil, vinegar, coriander and mint.

Put the ribs and marinade in a single layer on a baking sheet and cook in the preheated oven for 30 minutes. Turn the ribs and return them to the oven for a further 10–15 minutes. (If the ribs start to stick to the sheet in the final few minutes of cooking, reduce the temperature to 180°C (350°F) Gas 4.) Serve with the salsa and any remaining marinade spooned over.

250 ml maple syrup

95 g soft brown sugar

375 ml cider vinegar

125 ml Thai fish sauce

2 garlic cloves

10–12 large dried red chillies (Kashmiri)

8 long spare ribs, ideally 10–15 cm

corn salsa

3 tablespoons light olive oil

2 fresh corn-on-the-cobs, shucked

1 small red onion, chopped

1 large red chilli, deseeded and finely chopped

2 tablespoons red wine vinegar

1 small bunch of fresh coriander, chopped

1 large handful of fresh mint leaves, chopped

serves 4

sweet temptations

blueberry sour cream pancakes with maple syrup pecans • breakfast doughnuts • scones with clotted cream and strawberry jam • bird's nest cupcakes • cranberry and dark chocolate brownies • chocolate fudge cookies • bread and butter puddings • sticky toffee pudding • old english trifle • chocolate mousse • crème caramel • new york cheesecake • mississippi mud pie • strawberry shortcake • blackberry crumble • dusky apple pie • banana splits with hot fudge sauce • raspberries-and-cream layer cake • carrot and walnut cake with cream cheese filling

A delicious treat with an all-American flavour, these pancakes will disappear as fast as you can put them on the table. You can make the pancakes with either fresh or frozen berries. The frozen ones take slightly longer to cook and so are less likely to burn.

blueberry sour cream pancakes with maple syrup pecans

Preheat the oven to 200°C (400°F) Gas 6.

To make the maple syrup pecans, spread the nuts over a baking sheet and cook in the preheated oven for 5 minutes until lightly toasted. Simmer the maple syrup in a small saucepan for 3 minutes. Remove from the heat and stir in the pecans and butter.

To make the pancakes, sift the flour, baking powder, salt and sugar into a bowl. Put the egg yolks, sour cream, milk and butter into a second bowl and beat well, then add the flour mixture all at once and beat until smooth. Put the egg whites into a clean bowl and whisk until soft peaks form. Fold them gently into the batter, then fold in the blueberries. Do not overmix – a few lumps of flour and egg white don't matter.

Heat the prepared griddle over medium heat. Reduce the heat. Pour 3 tablespoons of batter into the pan and cook in batches of 3–4 for 1–2 minutes over very low heat to avoid burning the blueberries, until small bubbles begin to appear on top and the underside is golden brown. Turn them over and cook the other side for 1 minute. Transfer to a plate and keep them warm in a low oven while you cook the remainder.

Serve with good vanilla ice cream and the maple syrup pecans.

285 g plain flour

2 teaspoons baking powder

1 teaspoon salt

55 g caster sugar

2 eggs, separated

250 ml sour cream

150 ml milk

55 g unsalted butter, melted and cooled

250 g blueberries, fresh or frozen

vanilla ice cream, to serve

maple syrup pecans

100 g pecan halves

250 ml maple syrup

55 g unsalted butter

a baking sheet

a flat griddle pan or frying pan, preheated and lightly greased

makes 8–10 pancakes

Doughnuts with coffee are a time-honoured mid-morning snack, but made to this recipe they are substantial enough to eat for breakfast. Rather than a yeast dough, these use mashed floury potatoes for speed and flavour. They are best eaten freshly made and still warm.

breakfast doughnuts

Mix the flour with the salt, spices, bicarbonate of soda and sugar in a large bowl. Rub in the butter with the tips of your fingers until the mixture looks like crumbs.

Add the mashed potatoes, work in briefly, then work in the eggs and enough of the buttermilk to make a soft, scone-like dough. If the dough feels very sticky, work in extra flour, adding 1 tablespoon at a time.

Turn out the dough onto a lightly floured work surface and knead for a few seconds until it is just smooth. Roll it out 1.5 cm thick, then cut out rounds using the larger cutter. Stamp out the centre of each round with the smaller cutter.

Re-roll the trimmings and centre circles, then cut out more rings.

Fill a chip pan one-third full with the oil (or a deep-fat fryer to the manufacturer's recommended level). Heat the oil to 180°C (350°F), or until a small cube of bread turns brown in 40 seconds. Fry the doughnuts 2 or 3 at a time, turning them frequently until well browned and cooked through, about 4 minutes. Remove from the oil with a slotted spoon and drain well on kitchen paper.

Mix the cinnamon sugar ingredients together, sprinkle over the doughnuts, then serve warm with coffee.

Best eaten within 24 hours.

450 g plain flour

¼ teaspoon sea salt

½ teaspoon ground ginger

½ teaspoon ground cinnamon

½ teaspoon freshly grated nutmeg

1½ teaspoons bicarbonate of soda

200 g golden caster sugar

40 g unsalted butter, cubed

225 g very smooth mashed potatoes (page 31)

2 medium eggs, beaten

230 ml buttermilk (or a mixture of half plain yoghurt and half semi-skimmed milk)

vegetable oil, for deep-frying

cinnamon sugar

2 tablespoons caster sugar

1 teaspoon ground cinnamon

a large chip pan or saucepan, or an electric deep-fryer

8-cm round plain biscuit cutter

2-cm round plain biscuit cutter

makes 12 doughnuts

Traditionally served with clotted cream and rich, fruity jam, these classic scones are a must for the family tea table. Some people put the jam on first, followed by a dollop of cream; others argue for putting the cream on first. For real luxury, use homemade strawberry jam (page 173).

scones with clotted cream and strawberry jam

Preheat the oven to 220°C (425°F) Gas 7.

Put the flour, baking powder and sugar in a food processor and pulse to combine. Add the butter and process for about 20 seconds until the mixture resembles fine breadcrumbs. Transfer to a large bowl and make a well in the centre.

Beat together the egg and milk in another bowl, reserving 1 tablespoon of the mixture in a separate bowl. Pour most of the remaining liquid into the flour mixture and bring together into a soft dough using a fork. If there are still dry crumbs, add a little more of the liquid. Turn out onto a lightly floured surface and knead briefly until smooth. Work in a little more flour if the mixture is sticky. Gently pat or roll out the dough to about 2.5 cm thick and cut out rounds using the biscuit cutter, pressing the trimmings together to make more scones.

Arrange the scones on a greased baking sheet, spacing them slightly apart, and glaze the tops with the reserved egg and milk mixture. Bake for about 8 minutes, or until risen and golden. Transfer to a wire rack to cool slightly. Serve warm with clotted cream and strawberry jam.

225 g self-raising flour

1 teaspoon baking powder

2 tablespoons caster sugar

50 g unsalted butter, chilled and cubed

1 egg

75 ml milk

to serve

clotted cream

good-quality strawberry jam

a 4-cm or 5-cm biscuit cutter

makes 10–12 scones

Children love these little chocolate nests with pretty pastel-coloured eggs nestling inside. They're easy to make and kids will have a great time helping to decorate them – perfect if you're looking for a fun activity on a rainy afternoon. The eggs make them a good choice for a sweet treat at Easter time, but you can enjoy them at any season.

bird's nest cupcakes

Preheat the oven to 180°C (350°F) Gas 4.

Beat the butter and sugar together in a bowl until pale and fluffy, then beat in the eggs, one at a time. Sift the flour and cocoa powder into the mixture and fold in, then stir in the milk.

Spoon the mixture into the paper cases and bake in the preheated oven for 18 minutes until risen and a skewer inserted in the centre comes out clean. Transfer to a wire rack to cool.

To decorate, put the mascarpone, icing sugar and cocoa powder in a bowl and beat together until smooth and creamy. Pop a dollop of icing on top of each cake.

Break the chocolate flake bars into shards resembling twigs, then arrange them on top of the icing to create 12 little bird's nests. Finish off with three eggs in the centre of each nest.

115 g unsalted butter, at room temperature

115 g caster sugar

2 eggs

115 g self-raising flour

1½ tablespoons cocoa powder

2 tablespoons milk

to decorate

150 g mascarpone

50 g icing sugar, sifted

1 tablespoon cocoa powder

2–3 chocolate flake bars

36 sugar-coated chocolate eggs (about 100 g)

a 12-hole cupcake tin, lined with paper cases

makes 12 cupcakes

The sharpness of dried cranberries balances the sweetness of this dark chocolate brownie mixture, and the tangy grated orange zest lifts the richness. These sophisticated brownies will keep moist for up to 5 days, though there's not much chance of them staying uneaten that long!

cranberry and dark chocolate brownies

Preheat the oven to 180°C (350°F) Gas 4.

Break up the chocolate and put it in a heatproof mixing bowl with the butter. Set the bowl over a pan of steaming water and melt gently, stirring frequently. Remove the bowl from the pan and leave to cool until needed.

Whisk the eggs until frothy using an electric mixer or whisk. Add the sugar and orange zest and whisk until the mixture becomes very thick and mousse-like. Whisk in the melted chocolate.

Sift the flour onto the mixture and stir in. When everything is thoroughly combined stir in the dried cranberries. Transfer the mixture to the prepared tin and spread evenly.

Bake in the preheated oven for about 25 minutes or until a skewer inserted halfway between the sides and the centre comes out just clean. Remove the tin from the oven.

Leave to cool before removing from the tin and cutting into 20 pieces. Store in an airtight container and eat within 5 days.

200 g good-quality plain chocolate

200 g unsalted butter, cubed

3 large free-range eggs

175 g caster sugar

grated zest of 1 medium unwaxed orange

200 g plain flour

100 g dried cranberries

a brownie tin, 20.5 x 25.5 cm, greased and base-lined

makes 20 brownies

This very quick recipe uses a food processor. Plain chocolate gives the cookies a rich flavour. They are excellent for serving with a good vanilla ice cream and can be enjoyed at any time with a cup of coffee.

chocolate fudge cookies

Preheat the oven to 180°C (350°F) Gas 4.

Put both the sugars in a food processor. Add the pieces of chocolate, then process until the mixture has a sandy texture.

Add the pieces of butter, flour, baking powder and egg and process until the mixture comes together to make a firm dough. Carefully remove from the machine.

Lightly flour your hands and roll the dough into about 20 walnut-sized balls. Arrange them, spaced well apart, on the prepared sheets.

Bake in the preheated oven for 12–15 minutes until firm.

Let cool on the sheets for 2 minutes, then transfer to wire racks to cool completely.

Store in an airtight container and eat within 5 days or freeze for up to a month.

variation: Remove the dough from the processor and work in 75 g pecan pieces, then shape and bake the cookies as above.

75 g caster sugar

75 g light muscovado sugar

140 g good plain chocolate, broken up

110 g unsalted butter, chilled and cubed

150 g plain flour

½ teaspoon baking powder

1 large egg, lightly beaten

several baking sheets, greased

makes about 20

Bread and butter pudding is a childhood favourite for many people – but grown-ups love it, too. This simple dish is enjoying something of a revival at the moment. There are various ways of making it, and here tea cakes are used instead of ordinary bread. Taking less than 20 minutes to cook, this pudding is served in individual dishes.

bread and butter puddings

Preheat the oven to 180°C (350°F) Gas 4.

Put the milk, cream, vanilla extract and 3 tablespoons of the sugar into a saucepan and heat until the sugar dissolves.

Put the eggs into a bowl, whisk well, stir in 2–3 tablespoons of the hot milk mixture to warm the eggs, then stir in the remainder of the hot milk.

Lightly toast the tea cakes and cut into quarters. Divide between the prepared dishes and sprinkle with the sultanas.

Pour in the custard, grate a little nutmeg over the top, then sprinkle with the remaining sugar. Bake for 18–20 minutes, or until firm. Leave to cool a little, then serve warm.

300 ml milk

300 ml double cream

½ teaspoon vanilla extract

4 tablespoons caster sugar

3 eggs

6 tea cakes or hot cross buns, halved

50 g sultanas

1 whole nutmeg

6 individual dishes, 200 ml each, well greased

serves 6

This is the sort of gloriously sticky pudding that really does leave happy memories. It can be mixed, baked in the oven and placed on the table in under an hour. The toffee sauce is also good poured over ice cream.

sticky toffee pudding

Preheat the oven to 180°C (350°F) Gas 4.

To make the pudding, put the dates and the boiling water in a small saucepan or heatproof bowl, then stir in the bicarbonate of soda and leave to soak until needed.

Put the butter in a mixing bowl or the bowl of an electric mixer. Add the sugar and vanilla extract and beat until very well combined (the mixture won't look soft and fluffy like a sponge cake mix).

Pour a little of the beaten egg into the mixing bowl and beat well. Keep on adding the eggs, a little at a time, then beating well, until all the eggs have been used up.

Sift the flour and baking powder into the bowl. Stir gently a few times to half-mix in the flour, then pour the date and water mixture into the bowl. Carefully mix the whole lot together to make a runny batter.

Pour the batter into the prepared baking dish and bake for 40–45 minutes, or until golden brown. A skewer inserted into the centre should come out clean. If not, give the pudding another 5 minutes in the oven before testing again.

While the pudding is baking, make the toffee sauce. Put the sugar, butter and cream in a small saucepan. Set the pan over low heat and heat gently, stirring now and then until melted, smooth and hot. Remove the pudding from the oven and serve warm with the hot toffee sauce. Any leftover pudding and sauce can be gently reheated and served again. Eat within 2 days.

175 g stoned dates, chopped

300 ml boiling water

1 teaspoon bicarbonate of soda

50 g unsalted butter, softened

175 g caster sugar

½ teaspoon vanilla extract

2 large free-range eggs, at room temperature, beaten

225 g plain flour

1 teaspoon baking powder

toffee sauce

100 g dark brown muscovado sugar

50 g unsalted butter

200 ml single cream

an ovenproof baking dish, about 1.5 litre capacity, greased

makes 1 large pudding

Sponge cakes soaked in sherry and topped with fruit, homemade egg custard and cream, create this delicious trifle, which everyone will adore. Try tinned apricots instead of peaches or 350–400 g thinly sliced Madeira cake instead of the trifle sponge cakes.

old english trifle

Spread the top of the sponge cakes with jam, then cut them into fingers. Arrange over the base of the serving bowl, covering the base completely. Sprinkle the crushed ratafia biscuits evenly over the top.

Drain the peaches, reserving the juice. Mix together the peach juice and sherry, then pour evenly over the sponge cakes and ratafia biscuits. Arrange the peaches in an even layer over the top. Cover and refrigerate.

Meanwhile, put the cornflour in a heatproof bowl, add 3 tablespoons of the milk and blend together with a whisk until smooth. Add the egg yolks, sugar and vanilla extract and whisk together to mix. Set aside.

Pour the remaining milk in a saucepan and heat gently until almost boiling. Pour the hot milk onto the egg yolk mixture, whisking constantly. Return the mixture to the pan, then cook gently, stirring continuously, until the mixture thickens enough to coat the back of a wooden spoon. Do not allow the mixture to boil as it may curdle.

Remove the pan from the heat and pour the custard into a heatproof bowl. Cover the surface of the hot custard with a piece of greaseproof paper (to prevent a skin forming) and leave to cool completely.

Spoon the cold custard over the peach layer. Lightly whip the cream until it forms soft peaks, then spread cream over the custard, covering it completely. Cover and refrigerate for 3–4 hours before serving. Sprinkle the cream with the flaked almonds, then serve.

8 trifle sponge cakes

115 g raspberry jam

100 g ratafia biscuits or amaretti, lightly crushed

415 g tinned peach slices in fruit juice

100 ml sherry

1 tablespoon cornflour

600 ml whole milk

4 egg yolks

55 g castor sugar

1 teaspoon vanilla extract

300 ml double cream

40 g toasted flaked almonds

a deep glass serving bowl

serves 8

This is very easy to make and ideal for entertaining, since it should be made one day in advance. It is also deceptively rich, thanks to the egg yolks, which can be reduced in quantity or omitted altogether. It is important to use good-quality chocolate, but anything over 70 per cent cocoa solids will be too strongly flavoured.

chocolate mousse

Put the chocolate in a heatproof bowl and melt gently over a pan of steaming water. Alternatively, melt in the microwave on HIGH for 40 seconds, then stir and repeat until almost completely melted. Stir the butter into the melted chocolate. Using the tip of a small knife, scrape the small black seeds from the vanilla pod into the chocolate. Add the egg yolks, stir and set the mixture aside.

Using an electric mixer, beat the egg whites and salt until foaming. Continue beating and add the sugar. Beat on high until glossy and firm.

Carefully fold the whites into the chocolate with a rubber spatula until no more white specks can be seen.

Transfer the mousse to serving dishes and refrigerate for at least 6 hours, but overnight is best. To serve, add a blob of crème fraîche on top of each mousse, or offer the crème in a separate bowl for people to help themselves.

200 g dark chocolate, broken into pieces

30 g unsalted butter, cut into small pieces

1 vanilla pod, split lengthways with a small sharp knife

3 eggs, separated

a pinch of salt

2 tablespoons caster sugar

sweetened crème fraîche or whipped cream, to serve (optional)

serves 4

Preparation of crème caramel is simple, and it is equally easy to eat!
There is a knack to turning out professional-looking custards. After baking,
leave them in their ramekins for 15 minutes before removing them from
the bain-marie. Run a knife around the inside edge of each ramekin, hold
an upturned plate over the top and flip over to release a perfect custard.

crème caramel

Preheat the oven to 180°C (350°F) Gas 4.

Put the milk, vanilla pod and its seeds in a
saucepan over medium heat and bring just to the
boil. Immediately remove from the heat, cover
and let stand while you make the caramel.

To make the caramel, put 100 g of the sugar, a
pinch of salt and 4 tablespoons water in a small,
heavy saucepan, preferably with a pouring lip.
Heat until the sugar turns a deep caramel colour,
then remove from the heat. When it stops
sizzling, pour carefully into the ramekins. Take
care not to let the caramel come into contact
with your skin; it is very hot. Set the ramekins in
a roasting tin and add enough boiling water to
the tin to come half-way up the sides of the
ramekins – this is called a bain-marie. Set aside.

Add the remaining 80 g sugar and another pinch
of salt to the saucepan of warm milk and stir
until dissolved. Remove the vanilla pod.

Put the eggs in another bowl and whisk until
smooth. Pour the warm milk into the eggs and
stir well. Ladle into the ramekins.

Carefully transfer the roasting tin with the
ramekins to the preheated oven and bake until
the custard has set and a knife inserted into the
middle comes out clean, about 20–25 minutes.
Serve at room temperature either in their
ramekins or inverted onto a plate so the caramel
forms a pool of sweet sauce round the custard.

750 ml full cream milk

1 vanilla pod, split lengthways with
a small sharp knife

180 g sugar

5 large eggs

salt

8 ramekin dishes

a roasting tin to hold the ramekins

serves 8

Traditional cheesecakes are often served with a thick fruit sauce on top.
This one is so dense and creamy that it really needs no embellishment.
If you like, simply smother the top with a selection of fresh soft fruit such
as raspberries, strawberries, blueberries, or cherries.

new york cheesecake

Preheat the oven to 140°C (275°F) Gas 1.

Crush the biscuits in a food processor then add
the melted butter and mix well. Press the mixture
firmly into the cake tin. Bake for 5 minutes,
remove and let cool. Grease the sides of the tin
above the crust.

In a large bowl, beat the cream cheese and sugar
with an electric whisk. Add the lemon zest and
juice, sour cream and vanilla extract. Mix until
smooth and add the eggs one at a time until well
combined. Put the flour in last and mix again.
Pour the mixture into the cake tin. Bake for
70 minutes until it is firm and the top is turning
light golden. Let sit in the oven with the door
open until cool (about 2 hours), then refrigerate
for at least 6 hours or overnight. Place your
favourite fresh fruit on top and serve.

200 g digestive or plain-chocolate
biscuits

60 g melted butter

1 kg cream cheese

250 g caster sugar

grated zest and freshly squeezed
juice of 1 unwaxed lemon

200 ml sour cream

2 tablespoons vanilla extract

5 eggs

4 tablespoons plain flour

a selection of fresh soft fruit

*a springform cake tin, about 20 cm
diameter*

serves 8–10

This famous pie from the south of the USA is supposed to look like the thick, dark, muddy waters of the Mississippi delta. It is very easy to make and is perfect for sharing with family and friends.

mississippi mud pie

Preheat the oven to 180°C (350°F) Gas 4.

To make the base, put the biscuits into a food processor and process until fine crumbs form. Alternatively, put the biscuits into a plastic bag and crush with a rolling pin. Transfer the crumbs to a mixing bowl.

Put the butter and chocolate into a heatproof bowl set over a small saucepan of steaming but not boiling water and melt gently (do not let the base of the bowl touch the water). Stir occasionally, until smooth. Remove from the heat, then stir into the biscuit crumbs. When well mixed, transfer to the prepared cake tin and, using the back of a spoon, press onto the base and about halfway up the sides of the tin. Chill while making the filling.

To make the filling, melt the chocolate and butter as above. Remove from the heat and let cool.

Put the eggs and sugars into a large mixing bowl and, using an electric whisk or mixer, whisk until thick and foamy. Whisk in the cream followed by the melted chocolate. Pour the mixture into the biscuit case and bake in the preheated oven for about 45 minutes until just firm. Leave to cool for a few minutes, then remove from the tin.

To make the chocolate cream, put the cream into a mixing bowl, then sift the cocoa and icing sugar on top and stir gently with a wooden spoon until blended. Cover and chill for 2 hours.

Serve at room temperature with the chocolate cream. The pie can be made up to 2 days in advance. Keep it well covered in the refrigerator and remove 30 minutes before serving.

225 g digestive or wheaten biscuits

60 g unsalted butter

60 g dark chocolate, finely chopped

filling

180 g dark chocolate, chopped

180 g unsalted butter, cubed

4 large eggs, beaten

90 g light muscovado sugar

90 g dark muscovado sugar

180 ml double cream

chocolate cream

140 ml double cream, well chilled

3 tablespoons unsweetened cocoa powder

40 g icing sugar

a springform cake tin, 23 cm diameter, well greased

serves 8

This luxurious pudding has a shell of rich but light cake – known as genoise – piled with chantilly cream and fruit. The secret of getting genoise to rise is to beat a lot of air into the mixture, so turn your mixer on to high and keep it going for at least 10–15 minutes. Don't wait for a party to try this recipe. Just make it whenever the family deserves a treat.

strawberry shortcake

Preheat the oven to 180°C (350°F) Gas 4.

To make the genoise, put the eggs and sugar in a bowl and beat with an electric mixer until light and fluffy. Using a spatula or whisk, fold in the flour until just blended. Transfer the mixture to the prepared tin and bake in the preheated oven until golden, about 20–25 minutes. Remove from the oven, unmould after 5 minutes and let cool on a wire rack.

To prepare the sugar syrup, mix the sugar and 5 tablespoons water in a small saucepan. Bring just to the boil and stir to dissolve the sugar. Remove from the heat and stir in the brandy. Set aside.

Put the strawberries in a bowl with a squeeze of lemon juice. Add 1 tablespoon of the sugar and toss to coat. Set aside. To make the chantilly cream, mix the remaining sugar and the cream in a bowl. Beat until it holds stiff peaks. Set aside.

Put the genoise on a board and, using a serrated knife, trace a circle around the top of the cake, about 2 cm from the edge. Cut down to 3 cm from the base; don't cut all the way through. Scoop out the middle of the cake and discard.

Set the cake shell on a serving plate. Using a brush, moisten the bottom of the cake with the sugar syrup. Spread a layer of chantilly in the bottom and add the strawberries. Using a flat knife, spread chantilly around the sides and over the top edge of the cake. Put the remaining chantilly into a piping bag and pipe rosettes around the rim. Refrigerate until ready to serve. This is best served on the day it is made.

4 large eggs

125 g caster sugar

125 g plain flour, sifted

filling

500–600 g strawberries, sliced if large, cut in half or quartered if small

freshly squeezed juice of ½ lemon

5 tablespoons caster sugar

500 ml whipping cream, chilled

sugar syrup

3 tablespoons caster sugar

1 tablespoon brandy

a deep cake tin, 23 cm diameter, lined with baking parchment and buttered generously

piping bag with fluted nozzle

serves 8–10

Fresh berries are so tasty and good just as they are that it's tempting not to fuss with them too much. That said, they are also very good used in a crumble – the tastiest of baked desserts. If you wait for the right season, you can organize a family outing to go blackberry picking. Fruit gathered from the hedgerows will have the best flavour of all.

blackberry crumble

Preheat the oven to 180°C (350°F) Gas 4.

Put the blackberries in a bowl with the caster sugar and the cornflour and toss to mix. Tumble the berries into the buttered baking dish and set aside for 15–20 minutes.

Put the plain flour and butter in a large bowl and, using the tips of your fingers, rub the butter into the flour until the mixture resembles coarse breadcrumbs. Stir in the brown sugar.

Sprinkle the mixture evenly over the berries and bake in the preheated oven for 45–50 minutes, until the top is golden brown.

Let the crumble cool slightly before serving with dollops of cream spooned on top.

375 g blackberries (about 2 punnets)

1 tablespoon caster sugar

1 teaspoon cornflour

130 g plain flour

75 g unsalted butter, cubed and chilled

60 g soft light brown sugar

double cream, to serve

a medium ovenproof dish, lightly buttered

serves 4

Apple pie must feature more often in people's memories of childhood than any other pudding. This one has a dark, spice-filled pastry that gives a delightfully different look and taste to a very old favourite.

dusky apple pie

Preheat the oven to 180°C (350°F) Gas 4 and put a baking sheet in the oven to heat up.

Put the apple slices in a saucepan with the lemon juice, lemon zest and sugar. Cover and cook over low heat for 15–20 minutes, turning the apples often so they soften and cook evenly. Set aside and let cool.

To make the pastry, put the flour, brown sugar and spices in a food processor and process for a few seconds to combine. With the motor running, add the butter several cubes at a time. Add the egg and 1–2 tablespoons of cold water and process until combined. The dough will look dry and crumbly. Transfer to a bowl and knead to form a ball. Wrap the ball in clingfilm and refrigerate for 30 minutes.

Cut the dough into two portions, with one slightly larger than the other. Roll the larger piece of dough between two sheets of greaseproof paper and use it to line the bottom and sides of the prepared tart tin. (Handle the pastry with care, as it will be quite crumbly.) Trim the edge of the pastry to fit the tin.

Spoon the apples on top of the pastry base. Roll the remaining pastry to a circle large enough to cover the base and place on top of the pie, trimming the edges to fit. Use a small sharp knife to make several slits in the pastry. Put the pie on the hot baking sheet and bake in the preheated oven for 50–55 minutes, until the pastry is dark brown. Remove the pie from the oven and let it rest for 15–20 minutes before cutting into wedges and serving with vanilla ice cream.

8 tart green apples (such as Granny Smith), peeled, cored and thinly sliced

2 teaspoons freshly squeezed lemon juice

2 thin slices of lemon zest

55 g caster sugar

pastry

250 g self-raising flour

185 g brown sugar

1 tablespoon ground cinnamon

1 tablespoon ground ginger

125 g cold butter, cut into cubes

1 egg, lightly beaten

vanilla ice cream, to serve (optional)

a loose-based fluted tart tin, 20 cm x 4 cm high, lightly greased

serves 8–10

Make these magnificent sweet creations to celebrate a special occasion or just to enjoy a sinful splurge. The combination of hot sauce, chilly ice cream, bananas, cherries and crunchy nuts is irresistible.

banana splits with hot fudge sauce

To make the hot fudge sauce, put the chocolate, cream and butter in a medium saucepan. When melted, add the golden syrup, vanilla extract and sugar, stirring constantly over medium heat. When nearly boiling, turn the heat down to low and simmer for 15 minutes without stirring. Leave to cool for 5 minutes before using.

To make the whipped cream, whisk the double cream with the sugar and vanilla extract and set aside. Cut the bananas in half lengthways. Take the pudding bowls and put 2 banana halves along the sides of each one. Put one scoop of each flavour of ice cream between the bananas. Top with one spoonful of the whipped cream, a sprinkling of pecan nuts and a cherry on top. Serve with a small jug of the hot fudge sauce to pour over the top.

4 small bananas, peeled

4 scoops each of strawberry, vanilla and chocolate ice cream

60 g shelled pecan nuts, chopped and toasted

4 maraschino cherries

hot fudge sauce

90 g dark chocolate, chopped

175 ml double cream

2 tablespoons butter

75 ml golden syrup

1 teaspoon vanilla extract

100 g caster sugar

whipped cream

250 ml double cream

1 tablespoon caster sugar

1 teaspoon vanilla extract

4 shallow pudding bowls

serves 4

A good cake for a party, this one looks wonderful and cuts easily. The vanilla sponge is baked in a rectangular tin, cut into two strips, then sandwiched with jam and topped with whipped cream and fresh berries.

raspberries-and-cream layer cake

Preheat the oven to 180°C (350°F) Gas 4.

To make the sponge, put the butter in a large bowl, then add the sugar, eggs, vanilla, milk, flour and baking powder. Beat with an electric mixer or whisk using medium speed. When very smooth and thoroughly blended, spoon the mixture into the prepared cake tin and spread evenly, right into the corners.

Bake in the preheated oven for 25 minutes, or until the sponge just springs back when gently pressed in the centre. Remove the tin from the oven and let cool for 10 minutes before turning out onto a wire rack to cool completely.

With a large, sharp knife or bread knife trim off the edges, then cut the sponge in half down its length to make 2 long strips.

Set 1 strip on a serving platter, then spread with the raspberry jam. Top with the second layer of sponge and press down gently. Whip the cream until very thick and soft peaks form, then spread over the top of the cake. Decorate with berries and serve.

Store in an airtight container in the refrigerator and eat within 3 days.

230 g unsalted butter, softened

230 g caster sugar

4 large eggs, at room temperature, beaten

½ teaspoon vanilla essence

1 tablespoon milk

230 g self-raising flour

½ teaspoon baking powder

filling and topping

5–6 tablespoons good-quality raspberry jam

225 ml double cream, chilled

450 g small fresh raspberries

a non-stick rectangular cake tin, 27 x 18 cm, or a roasting tin, greased

makes one 2-layer cake

Nearly every keen cook has a favourite carrot cake recipe. It's one of
those classics that can be made in an almost infinite variety of ways.
This version of carrot cake is crumbly and soft, and probably best eaten
with a spoon. If you are nervous about cutting the cake through the
centre, simply spread the filling over the top of the cooled cake instead.

carrot and walnut cake with cream cheese filling

Preheat the oven to 180°C (350°F) Gas 4.

Put the egg yolks and raw sugar in a large
bowl and beat for 2 minutes. Add the oil
and bicarbonate of soda and beat until just
combined. Fold in the flour, baking powder,
spices, carrot and walnuts until combined. The
mixture should look quite thick. In a separate
grease-free bowl, beat the egg whites with an
electric whisk until they form soft peaks then fold
them into the cake mixture in 2 batches. Spoon
the cake mixture into the prepared cake tin and
bake for 45–50 minutes, until golden and
slightly puffed on top. Let the cake cool in the
tin for about 10 minutes before turning it out
onto a wire rack.

To make the filling, put the cream cheese and
butter in a bowl and let them come to room
temperature. Add the brown sugar and, using an
electric whisk, beat for 5 minutes, until there are
no lumps and the beaters leave a trail when
turned off. Add the maple syrup a little at a time
and beat for a further 2 minutes, until the
mixture is smooth and a spreadable consistency.
Carefully slice the cooled cake in half and spread
the filling on the bottom layer.

2 eggs, separated

110 g raw (unrefined) sugar

200 ml light olive oil

1 teaspoon bicarbonate of soda

185 g plain flour

2 teaspoons baking powder

1 teaspoon ground cinnamon

¼ teaspoon freshly grated nutmeg

200 g grated carrot

100 g walnut halves

cream cheese filling

250 g cream cheese

125 g butter, cubed

3 tablespoons brown sugar

2–3 tablespoons maple syrup

*an 18-cm diameter springform cake tin,
lightly greased*

serves 8

sauces
& preserves

brown sauce • velouté sauce • hollandaise sauce •
barbecue sauce • gravy • mayonnaise • tartare sauce •
seafood sauce • bolognese sauce • pesto • caesar
dressing • french dressing • crème anglaise •
butterscotch sauce • chocolate sauce • granny's apple
chutney • chunky lemon, lime and grapefruit
marmalade • strawberry jam

This tangy sauce tastes nothing like the bottled variety you buy in supermarkets. It is traditionally served with meat, such as lamb or beef.

brown sauce

50 g smoked bacon, diced

25 g unsalted butter

2 shallots, finely chopped

1 carrot, finely chopped

100 g mushrooms, finely chopped

2 tablespoons plain flour

600 ml beef stock (page 40)

1 bouquet garni (page 41)

2 tablespoons tomato purée

1 tablespoon dry sherry

sea salt and freshly ground black pepper

makes approximately 300 ml

Heat a saucepan and stir-fry the bacon for 3–4 minutes, or until browned and the fat has rendered into the pan. Add the butter and fry the shallots, carrot and mushrooms for 8–10 minutes, or until browned.

Stir the flour into the pan and cook for 2 minutes. Remove the pan from the heat and gradually stir in the beef stock until smooth. Return the pan to the heat and bring the sauce slowly to the boil, stirring constantly. Add the bouquet garni, tomato purée and seasoning, partially cover the pan and simmer very gently for 50–60 minutes, skimming the surface occasionally to remove the scum.

Strain the sauce through a fine sieve into a clean saucepan, add the sherry and heat through. Serve hot or cool. To store, cover the surface of the hot sauce with clingfilm, leave to cool and refrigerate for up to 3 days.

Velouté, meaning 'velvety' in French, is made with stock and enriched with egg yolks or cream. A chicken stock is used here – which makes it the perfect sauce to serve with chicken dishes – but you could also make velouté sauce based on other light stocks, such as fish.

velouté sauce

Put the stock in a saucepan and bring to a gentle simmer. Meanwhile, melt the butter in another saucepan and stir in the flour. Cook over low heat for 2–3 minutes, or until golden. Remove the pan from the heat and whisk in the hot stock until combined.

Return the pan to the heat and bring to the boil, whisking constantly until the sauce thickens. Simmer gently for at least 20 minutes, skimming the surface from time to time. When the sauce is glossy, stir in the cream and warm through without letting it come to the boil. Serve hot.

500 ml chicken stock (page 41)

25 g unsalted butter

25 g plain flour

50 ml double cream

makes approximately 300 ml

Hollandaise is a smooth combination of butter, vinegar and eggs. Rich and creamy, this sauce is pure heaven when teamed up with such traditional partners as asparagus, artichokes or poached salmon.

hollandaise sauce

Melt the butter very gently in a small saucepan. Pour it into a small jug through a muslin-lined tea strainer to remove any excess milk solids.

Put the vinegar, shallot, salt and 1 tablespoon water in a small saucepan and heat gently until the liquid is almost totally evaporated, leaving only about 1 tablespoon. Remove from the heat and strain into a glass bowl.

Place the bowl over a saucepan of gently simmering water (do not let the bowl touch the water). Add the egg yolks and, using a balloon whisk, whisk the mixture for 2 minutes, or until pale and frothy. Remove from the heat.

Using an electric whisk, whisk in the melted butter, pouring it in in a slow, steady stream. Continue whisking until the sauce becomes thick and velvety. Serve warm.

150 g unsalted butter

2 tablespoons white wine vinegar

1 shallot, finely chopped

a pinch of sea salt

2 egg yolks

makes approximately 200 ml

variation: béarnaise sauce

Aromatic tarragon added to the basic hollandaise emulsion creates a classic sauce popularly served with pan-fried steak and frites.

Follow the method above for hollandaise sauce, but replace the white wine vinegar with the tarragon vinegar and add the tarragon sprig whilst reducing. Stir the chopped tarragon into the finished sauce.

2 tablespoons tarragon vinegar

1 fresh tarragon sprig

1 tablespoon chopped fresh tarragon

makes approximately 200 ml

A good barbecue sauce should be tangy, smoky and rich – just like this one. It's wonderful with homemade burgers (page 82) but you can also serve it with barbecued beef, lamb or chicken.

barbecue sauce

Put all the ingredients in a small saucepan, bring to the boil and simmer gently for 10–15 minutes, or until reduced slightly, and thickened. Season to taste. Pour into a sterilized bottle and refrigerate for up to 2 weeks.

note: Most supermarkets stock bottled passata.

200 ml passata (Italian sieved tomatoes, see note)

100 ml maple syrup

50 ml black treacle

50 ml tomato ketchup

50 ml malt vinegar

3 tablespoons Worcestershire sauce

1 tablespoon Dijon mustard

1 teaspoon garlic powder

a pinch of smoked paprika

sea salt and freshly ground black pepper

makes approximately 400 ml

The best gravy is made in the roasting pan whilst the cooked meat is left to rest. Gravy should complement the meat it is served with, not overpower it, and all you need is some pan juices, a little wine (white, red or even Madeira or port) and some stock or water and you'll have a perfect, delicately flavoured sauce to enhance your Sunday roast.

gravy

Pour off and discard as much of the fat from the roasting pan as possible, leaving just the lovely meat juices. Put the pan over medium heat.

Add the wine and scrape the flavoursome, sticky bits from the base of the pan. Boil for 1–2 minutes, then add the stock and simmer for a further 3–4 minutes, or until slightly reduced. Strain before serving with the cooked meat.

cooked beef, chicken, pork or lamb pan juices

100 ml white wine, red wine or Madeira

175 ml chicken stock (page 41) or beef stock (page 40)

serves 4–6

Making mayonnaise calls for a little patience and a steady hand with the olive oil, but it is worth the effort. Use a mild, pure olive oil rather than extra virgin olive oil, which can be overly harsh and bitter.

mayonnaise

3 egg yolks
2 teaspoons white wine vinegar
1 teaspoon Dijon mustard
300 ml olive oil
sea salt and freshly ground white pepper

makes approximately 300 ml

Put the egg yolks, vinegar, mustard and a little seasoning in a bowl. Using an electric whisk, whisk until the mixture is frothy. Very gradually whisk in the olive oil, a little at a time, mixing well after each addition until the sauce is thick and glossy and all the oil is incorporated. Cover the surface of the sauce with clingfilm and refrigerate for up to 3 days.

note: If the mayonnaise is too thick, then slowly whisk in 1–2 tablespoons boiling water to thin the sauce.

variation: *aïoli*

2–4 garlic cloves, peeled and crushed

Put the garlic in the bowl with the egg yolks, vinegar, mustard and seasoning, and continue to follow the recipe as above.

A bowl of fresh tartare sauce enhances any type of fish or seafood.
This sauce is simplicity itself to make.

tartare sauce

Combine all the ingredients in a bowl and season
to taste.

½ quantity mayonnaise (page 158)

1 tablespoon finely chopped spring onion

1 tablespoon capers in brine, drained and
chopped

1 tablespoon finely chopped gherkin

1 tablespoon chopped fresh flat leaf parsley

½ tablespoon chopped fresh dill

½ tablespoon snipped fresh chives

sea salt and freshly ground black pepper

serves 4

This is perfect for a lavish occasion. The rich tomato sauce infused with saffron provides a perfect base for fresh seafood, to serve with spaghetti or linguine. Saffron is not cheap, but you will need only a few threads – a very little goes a long way – and it's worth buying this aromatic spice for the flavour and rich colour that it adds to food.

seafood sauce

Heat the olive oil in a large, wide saucepan and gently fry the garlic and thyme for 3–4 minutes, or until soft but not browned. Add the tomatoes, stir well, then pour in the wine. Bring to the boil and simmer for 1 minute, then add the stock, saffron and seasoning. Cover and simmer over low heat for 30 minutes.

Meanwhile, prepare the shellfish. Cut the lobster tails lengthways down the centre of the back and discard any intestinal tract, then cut, through the shell, into 4–5 pieces. (You can leave the shell on or take it off before cooking – if you leave it on, warn guests to watch out for the shell in the sauce.) Wash the mussels in several changes of cold water, scrub the shells clean and pull out the straggly 'beard' if still attached. Cut away the tough grey muscle at the side of each scallop.

Add the lobster and mussels to the tomato sauce and cook for 5 minutes, or until the mussels open. Discard any that remain closed. Add the prawns and cook for a further 2 minutes, then add the scallops and cook for a further minute. Remove the pan from the heat and stir in the basil. Serve hot, drizzled with extra oil.

3 tablespoons extra virgin olive oil, plus extra to drizzle

2 garlic cloves, peeled and chopped

1 tablespoon chopped fresh thyme

625 g ripe tomatoes, skinned and finely chopped

150 ml dry white wine

150 ml fish stock (page 43)

a small pinch of saffron threads

2 x 350-g uncooked lobster tails

12 fresh mussels

12 large scallops

12 large uncooked tiger prawns, shelled and deveined

2 tablespoons chopped fresh basil

sea salt and freshly ground black pepper

serves 4

The addition of chicken livers gives an extra dimension to this classic sauce. Bolognese is quick and easy to prepare but needs slow cooking to allow the flavours to develop. Serve poured over freshly cooked spaghetti or use as the base for lasagne or other baked pasta dishes.

bolognese sauce

Heat a saucepan and dry-fry the pancetta for 3–4 minutes, or until browned and the fat is rendered into the pan. Remove from the pan with a slotted spoon and set aside.

Add the olive oil to the same pan and gently fry the onion, garlic and thyme for 10 minutes, or until softened. Increase the heat, add the mince and livers and stir-fry for 5 minutes, or until the meat is browned.

Add the wine and bring to the boil, then stir in the tinned tomatoes, tomato purée, sugar, bay leaves, fried pancetta and seasoning. Cover and simmer over low heat for 1–1½ hours, or until the sauce has thickened. Discard the bay leaves and season to taste.

125 g smoked pancetta, diced

2 tablespoons extra virgin olive oil

1 large onion, finely chopped

2 garlic cloves, peeled and finely chopped

1 tablespoon chopped fresh thyme

750 g beef mince

50 g chicken livers, diced

300 ml red wine

2 x 400-g tins chopped tomatoes

2 tablespoons tomato purée

a pinch of caster sugar

2 fresh bay leaves (or 1 dried)

sea salt and freshly ground black pepper

serves 4–6

This thick, aromatic herb and nut sauce is used throughout the world to serve with pasta or grilled fish, or be stirred into vegetable soup. It needs no cooking, the ingredients are simply blended together for a wonderfully fresh taste. Once made, cover the surface with a little extra olive oil, seal in a container and refrigerate for up to 3 days.

pesto

Put the basil, garlic, pine nuts and salt in a mortar and pound to form a fairly smooth paste. Add the olive oil slowly until you reach a texture that is soft but not runny. Add the Parmesan and pepper to taste. Cover the surface with a little olive oil and refrigerate for up to 3 days.

tip: You can make this sauce in a food processor, but do not over-process otherwise the sauce will become too smooth.

50 g fresh basil leaves

1 garlic clove, peeled and crushed

2 tablespoons pine nuts

a pinch of sea salt

6–8 tablespoons extra virgin olive oil

2 tablespoons freshly grated Parmesan cheese

freshly ground black pepper

makes approximately 150 ml

This is one of many variations on the original recipe for caesar salad dressing, first invented in the 1920s. Note that the ingredients include a raw egg yolk. If you prefer not to eat uncooked egg, you can follow an alternative recipe on page 21.

caesar dressing

Whisk the egg yolk in a small bowl with the garlic, anchovies, lemon juice, Worcestershire sauce and a little seasoning until frothy. Gradually whisk in the olive oil a little at a time until thick and glossy. Add 2 tablespoons water to thin the sauce and stir in the Parmesan. Store in a screw-top jar in the fridge and use the same day. Shake well before using.

1 egg yolk

1 small garlic clove, peeled and crushed

2 anchovy fillets in oil, drained and chopped

1 tablespoon freshly squeezed lemon juice

1 teaspoon Worcestershire sauce

150 ml extra virgin olive oil

25 g Parmesan cheese, freshly grated

sea salt and freshly ground black pepper

serves 4–6

This is a classic salad dressing with the perfect balance of flavours – it is neither too sharp nor too oily. It keeps for several days in a screw-top jar in the fridge. Always shake well before using.

french dressing

Combine the vinegar, mustard, sugar and seasoning in a bowl and stir until smooth. Gradually whisk in the olive and sunflower oils until amalgamated. Season to taste. Store in a screw-top jar in the fridge for up to 1 week. Shake well before use.

1 tablespoon white wine vinegar

1 teaspoon Dijon mustard

a pinch of sugar

4 tablespoons extra virgin olive oil

2 tablespoons sunflower oil

sea salt and freshly ground black pepper

serves 4–6

Crème anglaise – custard, by another name – should be stirred constantly over very gentle heat otherwise the egg yolks can curdle and spoil the texture. It is such a versatile sauce that it goes well with a variety of hot and cold puddings – most famously with apple pie.

crème anglaise

600 ml milk

1 vanilla pod, split

6 egg yolks

2 tablespoons caster sugar

serves 8–10

Put the milk and vanilla pod in a saucepan and set over very gentle heat until it reaches boiling point. Remove from the heat immediately and set aside to infuse for 20 minutes, then discard the vanilla pod.

Whisk the egg yolks and sugar together in a bowl until the mixture looks pale and creamy, then stir in the infused milk.

Return to the pan and cook, stirring constantly with a wooden spoon. Do not let the sauce boil.

When the mixture has thickened so that it coats the back of the spoon, remove from the heat. Serve hot, or if you prefer to serve it cold, cover the surface with clingfilm to prevent a skin forming, and leave to cool.

Butter, sugar and cream combine to make a wickedly rich toffee sauce,
ideal for drizzling over ice cream, steamed puddings and fruit.

butterscotch sauce

Melt the butter in a small saucepan. Add the
sugar and syrup and cook gently until the sugar
dissolves. Stir in the cream and vanilla extract
and slowly bring to the boil. Remove from the
heat and serve hot, or leave to cool and serve at
room temperature.

50 g unsalted butter

175 g soft light brown sugar

2 tablespoons golden syrup

75 ml double cream

a few drops of vanilla extract

serves 6–8

Use a good-quality chocolate containing at least 70% cocoa solids to
give a really rich, dark sauce – sublime with vanilla ice cream.

chocolate sauce

Combine the cream, chocolate and butter in a
bowl set over a saucepan of gently simmering
water (do not let the bowl touch the water). Stir
frequently until the chocolate has melted and the
mixture is smooth. Remove from the heat, leave
to cool for 10 minutes, then stir in the amaretto.
Serve warm.

175 ml single cream

150 g dark chocolate, chopped

15 g unsalted butter

1 tablespoon amaretto, or another
liqueur of your choice

serves 6–8

variation: white chocolate sauce

200 g white chocolate, chopped

175 ml single cream

Combine the chocolate and cream in a bowl set
over a saucepan of gently simmering water (do
not let the bowl touch the water). Stir frequently
until the chocolate has melted and the mixture is
smooth. Remove from the heat, leave to cool for
10 minutes and serve warm.

This is the sort of recipe that is kept alive by being passed down through generations of family cooks. The best thing is, like most chutneys, it is very simple to make. Serve in pork sandwiches, with all kinds of eggs, cheese, cold meats or cooked breakfasts.

granny's apple chutney

Chop the apples and onions very finely – this can be done in a food processor, but take care not to reduce it a pulp. It is important for the chutney to have texture.

Put the apples, onions, raisins, sultanas, sugar, cayenne, mustard, ginger, salt and the 500 ml vinegar in a large pan and simmer for 1–1½ hours over low to medium heat. Stir regularly to make sure the sugar does not burn, adding extra vinegar as necessary as the chutney reduces.

Turn off the heat and let the chutney settle. Stir and pack into the sterilized jars, cover with a waxed disc and seal at once. Label when cooled.

Keep at least 1 month before you try it. This kind of chutney improves with age.

note: To sterilize jars, wash them in hot soapy water and rinse in boiling water. Place in a large pan and cover with hot water, then cover the pan with a lid. Bring the water to the boil and continue boiling for 15 minutes. Turn off the heat and leave the jars in the hot water until just before you fill them. Sterilize the lids by boiling for 5 minutes, or according to the manufacturer's instructions.

1 kg cooking apples, peeled and cored

500 g onions, quartered

125 g raisins

125 g sultanas

500 g demerara sugar

½ teaspoon cayenne pepper

½ teaspoon hot dry mustard

½ teaspoon ground ginger

25 g salt

500 ml malt vinegar, plus 500 ml extra to add as the chutney boils down

4–6 sterilized jars, 375 g each, with lids or covers

waxed paper discs

makes 1.5–2.25 kg

Marmalade epitomizes leisurely weekend breakfasts in warm sunny kitchens. The beauty of this tangy marmalade, which uses three different fruits, is that it can be made in small quantities at any time of the year, not just when the Seville oranges are in season.

chunky lemon, lime and grapefruit marmalade

Scrub the fruit and prise out any stalk ends. Put in a pan and cover with 500 ml water. Set over low heat and cook until tender, 1½–2 hours.

Put the fruit on a chopping board to cool. Then cut in half, scrape out the flesh and pips and add to the pan. Bring to the boil and simmer for 5 minutes. Cut the zest into strips. Strain the water from the pips and flesh and return the pulp to the pan, adding the zest and lemon juice. Discard the pips and debris.

Add the sugar to the pan and bring slowly to simmering point, stirring until the sugar has dissolved. When the marmalade has become translucent, you will know the sugar has dissolved. Bring to the boil and boil rapidly until setting point is reached, 5–10 minutes.

Take the pan off the heat and test for set (see note). If the marmalade is not ready, return the pan to the heat to boil for a few more minutes and test again. When setting point has been reached, return to simmering point, then turn off the heat. Skim with a perforated skimmer, stir well and leave to stand for 30 minutes. Stir and ladle into the sterilized jars, seal with waxed paper discs and cover with a lid. Leave to cool, label and store in a cool, dark cupboard.

note: To test for set, drop a teaspoon of marmalade onto a saucer that has been chilled in the refrigerator. Leave for 5 minutes. Push it with a finger – if it crinkles it is ready.

1 unwaxed lemon

1 small unwaxed pink grapefruit

1 unwaxed lime

freshly squeezed juice of ½ lemon

1 kg sugar

3 sterilized jam jars, 250 g each, with lids or covers (see note, page 169)

waxed paper discs

makes 500–750 g

Jam-making doesn't have to be as time consuming or complicated as many people think. This fruit-packed strawberry jam is quick and simple to make – and will fill your kitchen with a wonderful scent. Eat it with hot toast or scones and clotted cream (page 117).

strawberry jam

Wash the fruit and pat dry. Hull the strawberries and discard any that are damaged. Put in a large pan and cook gently over very low heat for a few minutes to start the juices running. Take care not to let the fruit burn. Let stand overnight. If you like, the fruit can be mashed at this stage.

Add the lemon juice and sugar to the fruit and bring to simmering point over low heat. Stir well while the sugar is dissolving. When the sugar has dissolved, increase the heat and boil rapidly for 10 minutes (remember to stir occasionally to make sure the pan does not burn), until the juice has reduced and the jam starts to thicken.

Take the pan off the heat and test for set (see note). If the jam is not ready, put the pan back on the heat to boil for a few minutes longer and test again. Repeat this process if necessary and remember to take the jam off the heat while testing, because over-boiling will ruin it.

When setting point has been reached, skim the jam with a perforated skimmer, stir it well and let stand for 20 minutes for the fruit to settle. Stir and ladle into the sterilized jars. Seal at once with waxed paper discs, wiping the necks of the jars with a clean, damp cloth if necessary. Close with a lid or appropriate cover. Let cool, label and keep stored in a cool, dark cupboard.

note: To test for set, drop a teaspoon of jam onto a saucer that has been chilled in the refrigerator. Leave for 5 minutes. Push it with a finger – if it crinkles it is ready.

1 kg small strawberries, picked in dry weather

freshly squeezed juice of 1 lemon

1 kg sugar

4 sterilized jam jars, 250 g each, with lids or covers (see note, page 169)

waxed paper discs

makes about 1 kg

index

recipe credits

Susannah Blake
Bird's Nest Cupcakes
Scones with Clotted Cream
and Strawberry Jam

Maxine Clark
Barbecued Sweetcorn
Leek and Potato Soup
Mashed Potatoes
Parmesan and Butter Risotto
Pizza Margherita
Quiche Lorraine
Ricotta, Basil and Cherry
Tomato Cannelloni
Roasted Mediterranean
Vegetables
Slow-roasted Tomatoes with
Garlic and Oregano

Linda Collister
Breakfast Doughnuts
Chocolate Fudge Cookies
Cranberry and Dark
Chocolate Brownies
Mississippi Mud Pie
Raspberries-and-cream Layer
Cake
Sticky Toffee Pudding

Ross Dobson
Blackberry Crumble
Carrot and Walnut Cake
Dusky Apple Pie

Sage Pork Chops
Scotch Broth
Smoky Sausage and Bean
Casserole
Sticky Spare Ribs
Tarragon, Chicken and Leek
Pot Pie
Upside-down Heirloom
Tomato Tart

Clare Ferguson
Cock-a-leekie

Tonia George
Beef Polpetti

Kate Habershon
Blueberry Sour Cream
Pancakes

Jennifer Joyce
Banana Splits
A Bowl of Red
Chicken Noodle Soup
Manhattan Clam Chowder
New York Cheesecake

Jane Noraika
Garlic Mushrooms

Elsa Petersen-Schepelern
Caesar Salad
Cream of Mushroom Soup

Greek Salad
Minestrone
Mixed Green Salad
Salad Niçoise
Tomato Soup

Louise Pickford
Barbecue Sauce
Beef Stock
Best-ever Beefburgers
Bolognese Sauce
Bread and Butter Puddings
Brown Sauce
Butterscotch Sauce
Caesar Dressing
Chicken Stock
Chocolate Sauce
Crème Anglaise
Fish Stock
French Dressing
Gravy
Hollandaise Sauce
Mayonnaise
Pesto
Seafood Sauce
Tartare Sauce
Vegetable Stock
Velouté Sauce

Anne Sheasby
Old English Trifle

Sonia Stevenson
Creole Gumbo
Traditional Fish Pie
Yorkshire Puddings and
Horseradish Sauce

Fran Warde
Beef and Carrot Casserole
with Cheesy Dumplings
Meat Loaf with Two Sauces
Roast Chicken with Lemon,
Thyme and Potato Stuffing
Roast Potatoes
Sausage and Bacon Toad-in-
the-hole

Laura Washburn
Chocolate Mousse
Cottage Pie
Crème Caramel
French Onion Soup
Macaroni Gratin
Ratatouille
Steak and Frites
Strawberry Shortcake
Wilted Greens

Lindy Wildsmith
Chunky Lemon, Lime and
Grapefruit Marmalade
Granny's Apple Chutney
Strawberry Jam

photography credits

Key: a=above, b=below,
r=right, l=left, c=centre.

Caroline Arber
Pages 2, 5br, 9, 30, 60, 90,
92, 95

Martin Brigdale
Pages 1, 5ar, 7, 12, 32, 50,
57, 58, 63, 64, 71, 72 80,
84, 86, 99, 103, 115, 116,
119, 128, 131, 132, 136,
139, 144

Peter Cassidy
Pages 5al, 11, 14, 16, 19,
20, 23, 28, 31, 45, 46, 53,
76, 124

Tara Fisher
Pages 168, 171, 172

Richard Jung
Pages 54, 67, 79, 89, 100,
104, 108, 110, 120, 140,
143, 148

William Lingwood
Pages 27, 68, 96, 112, 135

Diana Miller
Pages 123, 147

David Munns
Page 24

Noel Murphy
Pages 35, 36, 49, 107

William Reavell
Page 75

Yuki Sugiura
Pages 8, 38

Debi Treloar
Pages 4, 5bl, 13 inset

Ian Wallace
Pages 40, 42, 83, 150,
152–166

Polly Wreford
Pages 13 main, 127